BOB M
BIOGI

The Legendary Collaboration of Bob Marley and The Wailers

Jeremy Ray Hulburt

Biography

BOB MARLEY

The Legendary Collaboration of Bob Marley and The Wailers

CONTENTS

Timeline: Events in the Life of Bob Marley

CHAPTER 1

From Country Boy to Ghetto Youth

CHAPTER 2

Out of the Ghetto and into the Light

CHAPTER 3

Reach the world

CHAPTER 4

Reggae International

CHAPTER 5

Home to Mount Zion

CHAPTER 6

The Legend and the Legacy

CHAPTER 7

The marley family

Timeline: Events in the Life of Bob Marley

1945   Nesta Robert Marley, the only child of Cedella Mal-colm and Captain Norval Sinclair Marley, was born at 2:30 P.M. on February 6, 1945. The birth took place on Cedella's father's (Omeriah Malcolm) farm in Nine Mile, St. Ann's Parish, Jamaica. Bob stayed on this fam-ily farm until he was six.

1951   Bob went to live with his father in Kingston, Jamaica. When Cedella arrived the following year to look in on Bob, she discovered that he had not been living with his father but had instead been staying with an elderly woman named Mrs. Grey.

1952   Once mother and son were reunited, they returned to-gether to their rural Jamaican home in St. Ann.

1955   Bob learned that his father had died, and his mother moved to Kingston (without him) to earn a better living.

1956   Bob was moved from his grandfather's farm to live with his mother's sister, for whom he tended a herd of goats.

1957   Bob was reunited with his mother when he moved to Kingston to join her. This otherwise happy reunion was marred by the fact that they now lived in Kingston's west-side ghetto known as Trench Town.

1959   After attending several area schools, including Ebenezer, Wesley, and St. Aloysius, Bob ended his formal educa-tion when he quit school. He spent his time playing soccer, hanging out with other ghetto youth, and gradu-ally picking up music.

1960   Together with his closest friend Bunny, born Neville Livingston, Bob began to cultivate his musical talents. He and Bunny built rudimentary instruments and to-gether they practised singing by imitating Fats Domino, Louis Jordan, and the harmonies of Curtis Mayfield's Im-pressions. Also during this year, Bob and Bunny began studying singing with the Jamaican recording artist Joe Higgs. Higgs not only provided singing lessons, but he added Peter Tosh (born MacIntosh) to the group.

1962   At age 16, Bob was taken to sing for producer Leslie Kong, who issued his first recordings, "Judge Not," "One Cup of Coffee," and "Terror," on Beverley's imprint.

1963   Bob, Peter, and Bunny recorded for Clement "Coxsone" Dodd, who was one of the three biggest producers of Jamaican popular music on the island. Under the name The Wailing Wailers, the group released the single "Simmer Down," which brought them considerable suc-cess in Jamaica.

1965   The Wailing Wailers continued to have success with a series of solid-selling singles. By the end of the year, it was clear that Bob was the natural front man for the group. This led to friction that ultimately broke up the original three-member group. Early in the year, Bob met Rita Anderson (Alpharita Constantia Anderson), whom he soon married.

1966   Together, Bob and Rita had three children, although Bob had many other children outside his relationship with Rita. Later in this year, Bob moved to Wilming-ton, Delaware. Bob remained in Wilmington for seven months, during which time he worked a variety of odd jobs trying to make enough money to launch his own Jamaica-based record company. While in Wilming-ton, Bob stayed with his mother, who had previously relocated to the United States.

1969   Bob, Peter, and Bunny (under the name of the Wailers) recorded a series of successful singles for Johnny Nash and Danny Sims's JAD label. In the middle of the year, Bob was again in Delaware making and saving money to open his own studio in Jamaica.

1970   The Wailers begin recording a series of now classic singles for producer Lee "Scratch" Perry in what would be a legendary lineup: Bob Marley, Bunny Wailer, Peter Tosh, and the Barrett Brothers (Aston and Carlton) as the rhythm section.

1971   Bob, Peter, and Bunny, along with their rhythm section Aston and Carlton Barrett, were in London working for Nash and Sims on a record deal for CBS records. At the end of the year, the group was abandoned in London with no means to return to Jamaica. Bob made contact with Island Records' head, Christopher Blackwell, who fronted him the money to get the band back to Jamaica and make an album. This association quickly made Is-land Records the most important reggae music label.

1972   The Wailers released Catch a Fire, which was the first album-length recording of reggae music. The album had modest success and a degree of crossover appeal due to the rock and roll style guitar and keyboard overdubs that Blackwell added to the original tracks. In January 1973, the album was released in the United States and forever changed the way that reggae music was packaged and marketed. Catch a Fire was soon universally recognized as the first genuine reggae album in history.

1973   The Wailers launched their first official tour, which included television appearances on the Old Grey Whistle Test and Top Gear. Also in this year, the Wailers released their second record on the Island label, Burnin'.

1974   The Wailers reached international exposure due to Eric Clapton's cover of the Wailers song "I Shot the Sheriff." The song went to number one and sparked an enormous amount of interest in the reggae style. While they were experiencing the most success they had yet had, the original three-member Wailers core disbanded. Bob continued to use the Wailers name for the rest of his life. Without Peter and Bunny, Bob went on to release the Natty Dread album at the end of the year.

1975   In January, the original Wailers officially disbanded. The Natty Dread album was released internationally in Feb-ruary. Much of the summer and fall of the year was taken up by an international tour in support of the new album. Several shows were recorded in England and made into the first Wailers concert album, called Live! The album sold well in the UK and was released in the United States in 1976.

1976   Bob appeared on the cover of Rolling Stone magazine. Bob Marley and the Wailers released the Rastaman Vi-bration album then toured for three months to support the release. At approximately 8:45 P.M. On December 3, gunmen broke into Marley's house at 56 Hope Road and opened fire. Bob and Rita were each shot once and their manager, Don Taylor, was shot several times. Everyone survived, but this forced Bob into self-imposed exile in fear for his life.

1977   In the wake of the assassination attempt, Bob released a flurry of records. Exodus was issued on June 3, 1977.

1978   Kaya album released in early 1978. The Exodus and Kaya releases both spawned successful tours. Bob set up the Jamaican Peace Concert, which featured several important reggae acts. The concert was produced to help settle some of the violence that had been tearing the island apart.

1979   Bob and the Wailers released the Survival album in October of 1979. The album was another big success and led to another international tour which was launched in Boston at the end of October.

1980   The sessions that produced the Survival material also yielded the songs for the album Uprising. Uprising was released in June and was supported by another interna-tional tour with dates in the United States and Western Europe, during which the Wailers played for over one million people. During the North American leg of the Uprising tour, Bob collapsed while jogging in New York's Central Park. It was soon discovered that he had suf-fered a stroke and the rest of the tour was cancelled. The last live show that Bob Marley and the Wailers played was on September 23, 1980, at Pittsburgh's Stanley The-ater. In the wake of his collapse, Bob was diagnosed with terminal cancer in his stomach, lungs, and brain. At the end of the year, Bob travelled to Bad Wiessee, Germany, seeking nontraditional cancer treatment from Dr. Josef Issels. Dr. Issels was able to extend Bob's life, but could not successfully treat the cancer.

1980   On October 4, American popular musician Stevie Won-der released a tribute to the cancer-stricken reggae su-perstar. The song was reggae-like in style and was called "Master Blaster (Jammin')." It went on to be a serious hit on the U.S. rhythm and blues charts and topped out at number five on the pop charts.

1981   At 11:45 on Monday, May 11, 1981, Robert Nesta Marley, the first third-world musician who rose to international super stardom, died. In death, Bob was treated as a Jamaican national hero. He was awarded Jamaica's National Order of Merit and given a state funeral. Afterward, Bob's body was taken to his St. Ann's birth-place where it remains. Since his death, Bob's childhood home in St. Ann and his house at 56 Hope Road have become places of pilgrimage for ardent fans. Although there are many albums that have been released after Bob's death, the Confrontation album (released in 1983) was the only posthumous release that was conceived of by Bob before he died.

1984   The most popular collection of Bob's greatest hits, Leg-end, was released. The album went on to become the highest-selling reggae album of all time.

1999   The collection of Bob's greatest hits, Legend, received its 10th platinum certification, signifying that it had sold more than 10 million copies. This continues to easily hold the record for the highest-selling reggae boxed set

CHAPTER 1

From Country Boy to Ghetto Youth

Robert Nesta Marley was the first, and maybe the only, third-world superstar. Bob rose from humble rural beginnings to become a man of such significance and influence that his attempted assassination in 1976 was politically motivated. Bob's musical influence can still be felt today.

Despite his short life, at 36 years, Bob wrote an astonishing number of songs. And, unlike some songwriters, Bob was active in all areas of his music's composition. He worked on all of the musical sections, composed the lyrics, and was in the control room when the first tracks were laid down, as well as being engaged in the editing and overdubbing that resulted in the final product. Bob's sound was so distinctively reggae that it effectively monopolised the "roots reggae" label. His rhythm section invented the standard roots reggae beat, dubbed "one drop" rhythm. The drummer achieved one drop rhythm by accenting only the third beat of a four beat measure. Western European classical music traditionally stressed the first and third beats of a four-beat measure, but American rock and roll music emphasised beats two and four. This characteristic reggae rhythm distinguished it from the music from which it evolved and gave it a distinctly Jamaican flavour.

As well as the attraction that Bob's music had, he also had a very mag-netic personality. Bob was described as open, honest, and approachable, especially to his ghetto brothers and sisters. However, when deceived by a business associate or cornered by an interviewer, Bob could become quite nasty; he would quickly give the person a serious look that made everyone understand that he should not be taken for granted.

Bob's impact was felt during his life and continues to be felt today. Since 1991, Bob Marley and the Wailers have sold in excess of 21 million records (these statistics did not begin to be collected until 10 years after his death). Further, Bob has a star on the Hollywood Walk of Fame, he was inducted into the Rock and Roll Hall of Fame, he received the Grammy Lifetime Achievement Award, and he was awarded the Jamaican Order of Merit. Regardless of these (and many other) awards, the true test of Bob's worth is time. Twenty-five years after his death, the music of Bob Marley and the Wailers is as popular, important, and pertinent as it was the day it was released.

Bob was born in the island's rural interior, in the parish of St. Ann. Parishes in Jamaica are roughly equal to counties in the United States. Bob Marley was born in Kingston, Jamaica, to a black Jamaican mother, Cedella Malcolm, and a white Jamaican father, Captain Norval Sinclair (or Saint Clair) Marley. He then spent his days playing soccer, hanging out with his slum buddies, and getting into mischief. He also developed an interest in music. Another family in his tenement yard had a son named Neville O'Riley Livingston (b. 1947), known as Bunny. Bob and Bunny began performing cover versions of songs they had heard on the radio together, eventually making their own instruments out of various items. Their favourite possessions were a copper wire guitar, a sardine can, and a piece of bamboo.

While Bob aspired to be a great performer, Cedella was concerned about her high school dropout son. She was successful in getting Bob a position at a welding shop where he could learn a trade that would sustain him. While Bob never became a welder, the contacts he formed in the welding shop changed his life.

Bob followed his mother's instructions and worked in a welder's shop for a while, knowing that he required training to become a fine vocalist. He needed to learn the fundamentals of singing as well as the philosophy behind music composition. The man who could provide him with both of those abilities resided just around the corner from Bob and Bunny's yard on Second Street. Joe Higgs (1940-1999) was half of the popular pre-ska duet Higgs and Wilson. He had achieved popularity in the early 1960s and was a well-known figure on the Jamaican music scene. Higgs, however, chooses not to leave Trench Town, unlike other popular ghetto artists. Instead, he turned his Second Street yard into an impromptu music school where aspiring singers could take singing lessons.

Bob and Bunny started hanging out in Higgs' yard and soon learned how to sing in unison. Higgs also introduced the couple to Peter MacIntosh, a tall, slightly older ghetto teenager who went by the moniker Peter Tosh (1944-1987). Peter joined Bob and Bunny at Higgs' suggestion, making the group a trio. In addition, Peter was the only slum youth in Higgs' yard who owned a factory-made guitar, which he quickly taught Bob to play. The Teenagers were created by the three as a singing ensemble. The ensemble also had two female singers, Beverly Kelso and Cherry Smith, and was shortly joined by a fourth male singer, Junior Braithwaite. Because each singer's voice was in a distinct range, the trio worked effectively together to create vocal harmony. Bob sang tenor, Bunny performed a high falsetto naturally, and Peter sang bass. The ensemble covered songs by artists that influenced them, such as Sam Cooke, Ray Charles, and the Impressions.

Bob began creating his own songs in 1961, and the next logical step was to try to get them recorded. Bob decided to try his hand as a solo vocalist and approached Leslie Kong (1933-1971), a Chinese-Jamaican studio owner who refused to record the Teenagers. This time, Bob performed for Kong's newest sensation, 14-year-old vocalist Jimmy Cliff. Cliff was impressed enough by Bob's voice to persuade Kong to record a few of his tunes.

In 1962, Bob released "Judge Not," "One Cup of Coffee," and "Terror" on Kong's Beverley's label. Kong published these songs as 45-rpm singles, but they were not successful due to a lack of marketing and radio exposure. Bob was a renowned Jamaican recording artist at the age of 16. The three songs were thought to be originals composed by Bob at the time of their debut. Christopher Farley later discovered that "One Cup of Coffee" was a cover of a song by Claude Gray, an American singer/songwriter.

CHAPTER 2

Out of the Ghetto and into the Light

With the popularity of "Simmer Down," the Wailing Wailers became a Studio One fixture. They recorded frequently, and Dodd even let Bob reside in the studio. Living in Dodd's studio allowed Bob to spend hours practising the guitar. It also gave him the opportunity to listen to Dodd's rhythm and blues and soul records. Bob immersed himself in the Motown sound, spending hours listening to the output of the American southeast's soul studios.

The Wailing Wailers spent the mid-1960s performing live in addition to working in the studio. They were featured on Vere John's "Opportunity Hour" as well as the Ward Theater's "Battle of the Bands." Growing up in the slums, Bob earned the moniker "Tuff Gong" for his no-nonsense street demeanour. Bob lost his cool after losing one of these talent shows to a group called the Uniques. When the winner was announced, Bob erupted into a rage and challenged a member of the winning band to a fight.

Bob met female vocalist Rita Anderson (b. 1950) in early 1965. Rita was the leader of the Soulettes, a female vocal trio. Bob was harsh with the females at first, and they were terrified of him. However, Bob soon softened and revealed that he was attracted to Rita. Bob communicated his feelings for Rita by writing her love notes, which he had Bunny deliver. The two quickly became close, and the resulting love affair lasted the rest of Bob's brief life.

In early 1966, Bob planned a money-making excursion to Delaware. He did, however, make one condition: he wanted to marry Rita before leaving. Bob and Rita married on February 10, 1966. Friends of the couple hailed the wedding as the union of the island's two most promising singing ensembles. Bob, like his father, left Rita the day after the wedding to look for work in the United States.

Disillusioned with the Jamaican record industry once more, Bob planned another journey to Delaware to earn enough money to start his own record company and therefore keep control over the Wailers' work. Bob moved back in with his mother in the spring of 1969. This time, Bob worked at a Chrysler vehicle plant in addition to several other occupations. When he returned to Jamaica many months later, the money he had earned was used to sustain his family. Nonetheless, Bob was eager to return to the studio and brought the Wailers back to Studio One to work for Clement "Coxsone" Dodd. The second series of recordings with Dodd was much better than the first because Dodd had hired a new sound engineer, Lee "Scratch" Perry (b. 1936). The Wailers and Perry's collaboration was a success, and they created a distinct sound.

After completing their work on the Swedish film score, Bob and Nash proceeded to London, where Nash was attempting to secure a recording contract with CBS. When the agreement was reached, Bob brought the rest of the Wailers to London, where he assumed Sims was working on a similar deal for the Wailers. The Wailers recorded at CBS Studios as Nash's supporting band. While the Wailers did not receive a separate agreement, they did gain more recording expertise and returned to Jamaica with great aspirations for future English success.

The success of "Trench Town Rock" increased the Wailers' popularity throughout the island. It also signalled the end of insubstantial songwriting. In addition, the Wailers made big money from one of their hits for the first time. Bob and Rita used Bob's portion to open Tuff Gong Records, a record store where they sold

Wailers records. In addition to the proceeds from "Trench Town Rock," Perry continued to release Wailers singles and split the revenues with the band. Bob re-invested his portion and established Tuff Gong Productions to meet the growing demand for Wailers material. There was another burst of creativity that resulted in songs like "Satisfy My Soul," "Mr. Chatterbox," "Natural Mystic," "Concrete Jungle," and "Reggae on Broadway." Bob spent the remainder of his time writing new songs. He didn't like the quick pace or the weather in Delaware and was looking forward to seeing Rita and returning to Jamaica. Bob also began his conversion from Catholicism to Rastafarianism while in Delaware. His mother was horrified by the transformation, but she had no choice but to watch as Bob's hair grew into dreadlocks and he spoke more and more about Haile Selassie and Ethiopia.

Bob and the Wailers returned to England in the fall of 1971 to continue their search for a CBS contact for the Wailers. Bob and the Wailers embarked on a three-week CBS-sponsored tour with Nash's assistance. The Wailers' tour was successful, but it did not result in record sales. In the midst of this dire scenario, Bob took matters into his own hands and travelled to London to speak with Chris-topher Blackwell, the head of the Island Records Company. Following Bob and Blackwell's encounter, the record producer gave the band £8,000 sterling, which was enough to bring them back to Jamaica and back into the studio. In exchange for the money, Blackwell agreed to make a full-length reggae album with the Wailers.

"Jungle," "Slave Driver," "400 Years," "Stop That Train," "Baby We've Got a Date," "Stir It Up," "Kinky Reggae," "No More Trouble," and "Midnight Ravers" are some of the songs on the album. The format of the record itself was revolutionary. Reggae songs have previously been published as singles with an A and B side. With Catch a Fire, the format shifted to the long-playing record, allowing for better cohesiveness in the distribution of song blocks.

Rita gave birth to another boy in 1972, whom the Marleys named Stephen. With this new addition, the family relocated to a tiny house at Bull Bay, east of Kingston. This move marked a turning point in the Marley family's life; they had escaped the ghetto and would never return. Significantly, instead of returning to Bull Bay with Rita and the children each night, Bob frequently decided to stay in Kingston, at Blackwell's house at 56 Hope Road.

By 1973, Bob Marley and the Wailers had a successful album out with a major label and had mounted a tour of England and North Amer-ica. However, they still had not achieved the type of mainstream com-mercial success that Bob was convinced that they were capable of. The next step toward that success was taken with the November 1973 release of the band's second Island release, Burnin'. This release was less heavily modified by Blackwell and reflected the Wailers' interests in Rastafarian-ism and Jamaican politics.

The cover of the album was a silhouette of the six core Wailers' heads burned into the side of a wooden box. The picture included Bob, Peter, Bunny, the Barrett brothers, and Lindo, and the back of the record jacket had a large picture of Bob taking a drag off a large spliff. The tracks for this album were recorded at Harry J's in Kingston and mixed at the Island Records studios in London. The only musician on the album who was not pictured on the record's cover was the hand drummer Alvin "Seeco" Patterson. The album consisted of 10 tracks that included "Get Up, Stand Up," "Hallelujah Time," "I Shot the Sheriff," "Burnin' and Lootin'," "Put It On," "Small Axe," "Pass It On," "Duppy Conqueror," "One Foundation," and "Rasta Man Chant." This list represented some old and some new material.

Following the release of the album, the Wailers embarked on another tour to promote it. Bob and the Wailers joined the Sly and the Family Stone tour in the United States in an attempt to enhance the album's poor sales in the United States. Higgs replaced Bunny once more, as he had pledged not to tour following his ordeal on the Catch a Fire tour. This tour was a good break for the group because Sly and the Family Stone were already a popular band in America and were travelling following the success of their Fresh album. Unfortunately, the Wailers were dropped from the tour after only four performances. There were two reasons for the dismissal. For starters, the Wailers were supposedly outperforming the headliners, and the Sly and the Family Stone crowd was not fond of the Wailers' musical style. The Wailers were once again stranded in an unusual location due to the shooting.

With the band in disarray, Bob kept himself busy by working on the upcoming Wailers record. The third Wailers and Island release, Natty Dread, was the first without Peter and Bunny. The album marked a watershed moment for Bob, who was finally breaking out on his own as the band's primary songwriter. The I-Threes contributed vocal harmony in addition to Bob, the Barrett brothers, and Router. Lee Jaffe on harmonica and three horn players named Glen da Costa, David Madden, and Tommy McCook (the Zap Pow band's horn section) performed uncredited on the record. The Dread album cover was an airbrushed image of Bob alone in the centre of a multicoloured abstract background, while the reverse of the CD likewise featured Bob alone. The recording was done in Jamaica, like with previous Island Records releases, and the mixing was done in London, under Blackwell's meticulous supervision.

Natty Dread, released in 1974, was a mix of old and new tracks. The album included the songs ``Lively Up Yourself," "No Woman, No Cry," "Them Belly Full (But We Hungry)," "Rebel Music (Three O'Clock RoadBlock)," "So Jah Seh," "Natty Dread," "Bend Down Low," "Talkin' Blues," and "Revolution." The songs collected for this compilation most directly reflect Bob's interests, as they present Bob as a Rasta preacher preaching prophecy and revelation.

Undaunted, Bob Marley and the Wailers kicked off 1975 with a spectacular performance. When the Jackson Five performed in

Kingston, the Wailers were requested to open for them. This was Bob's first chance to really take centre stage and show off his charm and charisma. The visit, which also featured Al Anderson on lead guitar for the first time, was a big success. Natty Dread was formally published in February 1975 as the third Island/Wailers offering, and the album garnered favourable reviews from the UK and US press. The new and improved Wailers became an international success as a result of this success.

CHAPTER 3

Reach the world

Taylor, as the Wailers' manager, organised a huge North American tour as well as a small English tour for the band. The Wailers began the North American leg of their Natty Dread tour in June 1975. Bob established his on-again, off-again connection with the press during this tour. According to Bob's friends and bandmates, he rarely refused an interview, feeling that any press coverage was good for the band.

The Wailers concluded their North American tour with a performance at the Roxy Theatre on Sunset Strip in Los Angeles, California. Members of the Rolling Stones, as well as Cat Stevens, Joni Mitchell, Herbie Hancock, George Harrison and Ringo Starr of the Beatles, and members of the Grateful Dead and the Band, performed at the sold-out performance. This was an outstanding show of critical support for the Wailers. The gang believed they had made a good impact on the American audience, so they headed to London, ready to conquer another location.

Bob's final five years were spent constantly creating new songs, releasing seminal albums, and travelling in support of his efforts. The Wailers' popularity grew steadily, and by the end of the 1970s, the group was known even in the most remote parts of the world. Bob began his career in 1976 with a busy schedule of concerts, interviews, and recording. Bob's blossoming career reached a watershed moment when he appeared on the cover of Rolling Stone magazine, which named the Wailers "Band of the Year." Bob and the Wailers had also taken over the house at 56 Hope Road by 1976, despite the fact that Blackwell was still the formal owner. Early 1976 was spent recording new Wailers material and attempting to adjust to fame. Bob spent countless hours in interviews when the Wailers became international fame, attempting to describe to the world what it meant to be a Jamaican, a person of mixed race, and a Rastafarian.

In the middle of this upheaval, Bob Marley and the Wailers released their fourth Island Records album, Bob Marley and the Wailers, in May 1976. The CD was released with a front-of-the-album drawing of Bob. His dreadlocks had grown past his shoulders, and he was in a reflective position. The Rastafarian colours of red, yellow, black, and green were also strongly shown.The album jacket's background was burlap fabric, and it stated that the album jacket "is great for cleaning herbs." The other text was a phrase from the Blessing of Joseph in the Old Testament. Because Bob was a member of the Twelve Tribes of Israel Rastafarian cult, this text praised his strength and charity.

Rastaman Vibration was the Wailers' most successful album to date. It peaked at number eight on the US pop charts. Bob stated about the record that he was more interested with the message than the music. The songs on the CD cover a wide range of topics, from calls for revolution to political debates.The album's most significant Rastafarian song was "War." The lyrics of this song were adapted from a speech delivered by Haile Selassie at the United Nations on October 4, 1963. Selassie demanded equality for individuals of all colours, regardless of region or beliefs, in his speech.

The tour got underway at the Tower Theater in Upper Darby, Pennsylvania. Cedella Booker, Bob's mother, attended the show, and it was the first time she saw her son play live in concert. The Wailers then performed in Washington, DC, Massachusetts, and New York. They crossed into Canada for gigs in Montreal and Toronto before returning to the US for shows in Buffalo and Cleveland. The band then toured the Midwest before heading to Texas and completing the tour with seven performances in California. Following a stop in Miami, the band travelled to Western Europe, performing in Germany, Sweden, the Netherlands, France, and Wales. The tour came to a close with ten gigs in England. The Wailers played to sold-out crowds on the majority of their visits, and they were now performing to people who already knew the tunes.

Another peculiarity of the 1976 election was that, although Manley was courting Castro, the JLP's opposition leader, Edward Seaga, was accused of collaborating with the American CIA. This was ostensibly done to assist him in gaining control of the island, but it resulted in greater destabilisation of Jamaica, to the point where the island nearly broke into civil war in the mid-1970s. Everyone on the island was touched by the struggle for power between two Jamaican political leaders. Recognizing the harm being done, Bob recommended holding a concert for Jamaicans in order to thank the island's people for their support of the band. The "Smile Jamaica" Concert was set to take place on December 5, 1976, in Kingston's National Heroes Park. Bob needed the prime minister's office's clearance to hold such an event. This consent was obtained, but the PNP proclaimed the date of the next general election as December 20 in an act of pure political manoeuvre. In doing so, the PNP created the impression that Bob Marley and the Wailers were supporting the PNP's Michael Manley's reelection.

The violence of the 1976 election came right to Bob's 56 Hope Road house, thanks to the distorted view of the "Smile Jamaica" concert. Bob and the Wailers were rehearsing for their impending performance at the residence on Hope Road two days before the show. The band took a break, and one of the I-Threes, Judy Mowatt, requested that Bob arrange for someone to drive her home. Bob asked Gar-Rick to take the BMW and return Judy to her home because she was pregnant and not feeling well. Don Taylor was pulling into the 56 Hope Road driveway as they were leaving to supervise the practice. Bob, Taylor, and Kinsey were resting in the kitchen while waiting for Blackwell, who was supposed to meet Taylor there.

Taylor's car had been trailed into the driveway by two others who had gone unnoticed. Six gunmen escaped from these two vehicles and opened fire on the home. The kitchen was in the back of the house, up a few stairs. Bob, Taylor, and Kinsey heard gunshots and saw a gun barrel approaching through the kitchen door. As the gunman opened fire, everyone ducked for cover. Bob ducked for protection behind the refrigerator, but Taylor was left standing in the middle of the room. Taylor was riddled with bullets when the firing ceased; Bob had been shot once and the bullet was lodged in his left forearm; and Rita had been hit once in the head but the bullet did not puncture her skull. Lewis Simpson (or perhaps Lewis Griffiths—sources differ) was a Wailers associate who was severely injured.

Surprisingly, no one was murdered. Taylor was shot five times in the stomach and had to be airlifted to Miami for surgery. Both Rita and Bob were brought to the hospital for treatment. Rita was treated and released while wearing a bandage on her head. Bob was told that removing the bullet from his arm could cause him to lose feeling in his left hand. Bob declined to take the risk because he wrote his songs while playing the guitar, thus the bullet was left where it was. Overall, things could have gone a lot worse. The bullets that were fired into the kitchen were not precisely directed. Many of them, in fact, ricocheted throughout the room, leaving holes in the walls that can still be seen today. Everyone eventually recovered completely from their injuries over time.

Surprisingly, Jamaican Prime Minister Michael Manley paid Bob a visit when he was in the hospital. Manley placed Bob under the protection of the Jamaican security agency and escorted him away from the hospital. The prime minister was still preparing a Wailers presence at the "Smile Jamaica" Concert, thus shielding Bob was a form of self-protection. When Blackwell learned of the incident, he made his Strawberry Hill estate available to the injured Wailers. Strawberry Hill is located in the Blue Mountains in Jamaica's interior. Here, Bob spent the night trying to figure out what was going on and wondering about the future of his band, all while being heavily guarded by the government and local Rastas. Bob's thoughts were preoccupied with his injured friends and family, as well as if the band would still perform at the event.

With these, Bob was able to gather the band and monitor the situation in Kingston as he pondered the safety of performing the event. Bob quickly discovered that word of the attempted assassination had spread throughout the island. The supporting acts had all cancelled their appearances at the concert, putting the situation at Heroes Park in jeopardy. Bob found solace in the fact that his old friend Stephen "Cat" Coore of the band Third World was present, and that Coore's band had agreed to perform and test the waters. Bob decided to do the concert after much debate. Under heavy escort, he, Spaulding, and Rita rode down into the city and arrived at the site to discover 80,000 people waiting for the Wailers.

The band had already recorded 20 tracks before the second flurry of recording began, and they added another ten. The group then chose the ten most expressive tracks for the album, which was published on June 3, 1977, as the sixth Island Records/Wailers band offering. The songs on the album featured "Natural Mystic," "So Much Things to Say," "Guiltiness," "The Heathen," "Exodus," "Jamming," "Waiting in Vain," "Turn Your Lights Down Low," "Three Little Birds," and "One Love/People Get Ready." The lineup for the release was the same as for Rasta-man Vibration, with the exception of Marvin replacing Kinsey on guitar. The utilisation of a new drumming style from Jamaica was also featured on the record. The drumming method of uniformly accenting all beats in a measure, popularised by Sly Dunbar of the famed duet Sly and Robbie, developed songs known as "rockers," and the title track of the album was of this type.

Despite his injury, Bob and the Wailers continued their European tour. The band performed in Belgium, the Netherlands, and Denmark, as well as four gigs in Germany, two shows in Sweden, and five shows in England. The English gigs featured an appearance on Top of the Pops and four performances at the Rainbow Theatre. The Wailers' live presentation was even more exciting with Marvin in the band. Bob was suffering from his neglect to care for his wounded foot at the end of the London gigs. Bob's onstage dancing had reopened the toe injury, which had not been allowed to heal fully. Bob went to his mother's house in Delaware to rest after finishing the European leg on June 4 and the American leg not starting until the Palladium show in New York in July. Exodus had soared to number one on the English and German charts with the help of the tour, and the pressure was on to make the song a hit in the United States.

Bob's foot appeared to be worsening rather than improving, so he travelled to London to consult a foot specialist. The doctor examined Bob's foot thoroughly, including taking skin cells for examination under a microscope. The doctor then informed Bob that the sample indicated altered malignant cells, necessitating amputation of the damaged toe. Bob requested the doctor to look into alternatives, and he soon discovered that there was one, although it came with hazards. Instead of amputation, a tiny piece of the toe could be removed, and the wound cleansed and redressed. This option did not sit well with Bob, so he sought a second opinion in Miami.

Dr. William Bacon, who had operated on Taylor following the shooting at 56 Hope Road, examined Bob's toe. Bacon agreed with the London doctor that a portion of Bob's foot needed to be re-attached. The American portion of the Exodus tour was postponed on July 20 to allow Bob to have surgery. Although the tour was only officially postponed, all tickets were refunded and no dates were rescheduled. Bob's surgery was performed in Miami's Cedars of Lebanon Hospital, and all malignant cells were removed. Bob recovered at a house he bought in Miami after all of the altered cells were removed. The doctor recommended that Bob return to eating meat for protein as part of his recuperation. Bob was well enough to return to the road after two months of rehabilitation and a new diet.

The Wailers then embarked on a globe tour in promotion of the album. The tour was divided into three parts: two North American legs and one European leg. Another live CD was released as a result of the recording of many Wailers gigs from the Kaya tour.

Bob began the CD with an introduction in which he reiterated his trust in Haile Selassie I. In the name of Ras Tafari, he addressed the audience. He continued by saying that Selassie was "ever living" and "ever sure." Bob further identified himself with Selassie by using the Rastafarian phrase "I and I" several times. He then engaged the audience in a brief call and response, which led into the first track. The CD captured the Wailers at a new level of live performance, and the strength of Bob's singing and vocal presence demonstrated how much the vocalist had progressed since the Live! album three years before.

CHAPTER 4

Reggae International

The tour had been booked, and the Wailers were getting ready to embark on their maiden tour of the Far East and Pacific Rim. The tour's first two dates were slated for Abidjan, Ivory Coast. For unclear reasons, both of these dates were cancelled. Despite this initial disappointment, Bob continued to pursue Wailers engagements throughout Africa. The tour then began on April 5, 1979, with eight gigs in Japan. The Wailers flew from Japan to Auckland, New Zealand, for a performance. Bob was hailed by a group of Maori aborigines who treated him like a king and compared their struggles with an oppressive white government to those of the Jamaican underclass. Following the New Zealand exhibition, there was an eight-show stand in Australia. Following that, the band travelled to Hawaii for two gigs before returning to Jamaica.

Bob was now plotting his next move. He'd written many albums' worth of material in his thoughts while on the road. He was also preoccupied with organising a Wailers concert in Ethiopia. Bob decided that the Wailers' next big tour had to include an African appearance after spending long hours thinking about and debating the black fatherland. The continuing war between Ethiopia and the territory directly to the north known as Eritrea had impeded his efforts. Bob was unable to travel to Ethiopia due to the 30-year battle for Eritrean independence, which lasted from 1961 to 1991.

At the same time Bob was attempting to enter Ethiopia, Alan "Skill" Cole appeared in Addis Ababa, the Ethiopian capital. Cole had supposedly escaped to Africa in the aftermath of the Kingston assassination attempt. He'd utilised his soccer credentials to land a coaching position with the Ethiopian Airlines soccer squad. Bob was ultimately granted a visa in late 1978, and he and Cole planned a trip to Ethiopia together.

Bob flew from Jamaica to London, then to Nairobi, and finally to Ethiopia. Once there, he went to various places that were important to him, most notably those associated with Haile Selassie I. Bob also spent time on a religious community farm called Shashamane, attended a rally in Rhodesia in favour of the liberation effort, and enjoyed the local nightlife. Based on these experiences, Bob began work on "Zimbabwe," the African term for Rhodesia during the struggle for globally recognized independence from long-standing white minority rule.

Bob returned from Africa rejuvenated and eager to return to work. He had albums' worth of material ready for recording in his head, and his renewed conviction in black unity gave his new songs a serious edge. While he was overseas, his lawyer Diane Jobson oversaw the ever-expanding Tuff Gong enterprise. This was no easy task because she was in control of the sole multimillion-dollar music corporation in the third world.

The Wailers returned to the studio and released their first song, "Ambush in the Night." The song, which was published on the Tuff Gong label in early 1979, represented Bob's unwavering drive. Here, Bob addressed his would-be assassins once more, keeping them at bay since he was shielded by Selassie's divinity.

Bob was still conscious that the precarious post-One Love Freedom Concert calm had been broken, despite his busy schedule in the studio and with Tuff Gong business. Claudie Massop, an old acquaintance, was returning from a February social match when he was detained at a police roadblock. According to reports, Massop was unarmed when he approached authorities on the scene with his hands in the air. Officers opened fire, and Massop was shot 44 times, according to reports. The uneasy peace that had prevailed on the island since the One Love Peace Concert was disrupted by acts like these. The reasons for Massop's execution were never proven, however suspicions circulated that he stole money from the Peace event.

Lee "Scratch" Perry, another of Bob's long-time island buddies, had a nervous breakdown and was briefly institutionalised in Kingston's Bel-leview Hospital. Despite the tumult of 1979, Bob worked tirelessly to complete his next album. Another Wailers tour was already scheduled, and Bob wanted to finish recording the new songs before embarking on the trip. Even in the midst of the upheaval, Bob found some calm in his life during this time. He worked hard on his new record, but he also made time to play soccer and spend time with his children. He also had his 11th kid with Yvette Morris, a daughter named Makeba (the Queen of Sheba) Jahnesta.

Bob was introduced to a new Blackwell-assigned producer, Alex Sadkin, as part of the 1979 recording process. Sadkin began his career as an audio mastering engineer before moving on to become a well-known music producer at Criteria Studios in Miami and Blackwell's Compass Point Studios in Nassau, Bahamas. Despite his brief life (he died in a car accident in 1987 at the age of 35), he recorded tracks for the Talking Heads, Joe Cocker, James Brown, Marianne Faithfull, and others. His collaboration with Bob culminated in the album Survival. The album's working title, Black Survival, was inspired by Bob's journey to Africa and was released in the summer of 1979.

The CD itself had songs about resistance, faith, and fleeing oppression. The album, which contained ten songs in all, collected some of Bob's most personal reflections on his life and the world around him. The album's tunes included "So Much Trouble in the World," "Zimbabwe," "Top Rankin'," "Babylon System," "Survival," "Africa Unite," "One Drop," "Ride Natty Ride," "Ambush in the Night," and "Wake Up and Live." On this record, Bob was the Western world's downtrodden black man's leader. He sang about breaking the oppressors' chains and ushering in a new period of black liberation and global unity for the black race. He was a Rastafarian warlord on a quest to unite and bring peace to the African diaspora.

With the record completed, the Wailers embarked on another lengthy summer tour. They began the trip by headlining the Reggae Sunsplash II concert at Jarrett Park in Montego Bay in early July 1979. The Reggae Sunsplash concert series, which began in 1978, was partly Bob's brainchild. The Wailers would have undoubtedly taken part in the initial performance, but it took place while the group was away on the Kaya tour.

The Wailers were the appropriate headliners for the second version of the performance. Although rain turned the amphitheatre into a mud quagmire and limited the group's performance, the show was of historic proportions. The concert was a big success, drawing an international audience. The Reggae Sunsplash concert series is still going on today as a result of its success and international appeal. Every year, the top reggae talent from Jamaica is gathered for a performance on the island. This performance then acts as the kickoff to a lengthy tour promoting Jamaican music around the world.

The Reggae Sunsplash concerts have historically been hugely popular, introducing the globe to Jamaican music pioneers such as Third globe, Culture, Steel Pulse, Toots and the Maytals, Freddie McGregor, Morgan Heritage, Buju Banton, Beenie Man, Elephant Man, and others. When Tony Johnson, the primary force behind the performances, died in 1999, the series came to an end. The Reggae Sunsplash performance, on the other hand, returned with a three-day festival on August 3-6, 2006. The concert will be held annually again, and preparations for future festivals are already in the works.

With such a promising start, Bob Marley and the Wailers' 25-member Survival touring group left Jamaica for a lengthy American tour. The Wailers flew from Jamaica to Boston, Massachusetts, to perform at the Amandla Festival at Harvard University. Amandla is a shortened variant of the Shona term that means "power to the people" in Zimbabwe. Chester England created the Festival of Unity to help the Amandla group, whose purpose was to fund African liberation and freedom fighters. The event drew 25,000 people and featured celebrities from throughout the world, including American soul singer Patti Labelle. The Amandla show began with "Exodus" and concluded with "Zimbabwe" and "Wake Up and Live." Bob was the voice of African liberation throughout. During "Wake Up and Live," Bob began delivering a speech to the audience in which he discussed brotherhood, unity, and his concern for the conditions in Africa. The performance raised about a quarter-million dollars for African emancipation.

The tour then continued with a run of gigs in the United States, beginning with a stop at Madison Square Garden alongside the Commodores and rap icon Kurtis Blow. The band then performed for four days in New York's Apollo Theater. Bob had purposefully located this series of events in New York's traditionally black and lower-class neighbourhoods. Bob believed that by garnering the attention of Harlem inhabitants, his music could actually cross over to a black American audience. He soon became well-known in black American listening communities. The Survival album was officially released during this time period. Survival, in contrast to Kaya's commercial fare, was pure militant reggae and showcased Bob at his most potent. In addition to Bob's long-standing themes of black freedom in Jamaica, the new CD now contained discussions of black freedom in general, regardless of place. For the remainder of Bob's life, this Pan-African motif was woven into the fabric of his music and existence. Bob also continued to convey his message through his long-evolving predilection for Bible quotations.

Bob's convictions were reflected in the Survival CD. The album's front cover featured small-scale representations of all of Africa's flags from 1979. A banner at the top of the front cover depicted the pattern for stowing African slaves as they were transported in ships from Africa to the Americas. The title of the record was superimposed over this. The back cover retained the slave ship banner and added the song titles from the CD.

The album's lineup comprised the Wailers' previous recording's regulars. There was one notable addition, however: Carlton "Santa" Davis played drums on several crucial tracks. Davis had previously been a member of several of the island's most well-known bands, including Soul Syn-dicate. Since the 1970s, he has performed with nearly every prominent Jamaican popular group, including Jimmy Cliff, Black Uhuru, Burning Spear, Big Youth, Peter Tosh, Ini Kamoze, Big Mountain, and many others. During the Survival sessions, Santa sat in with the Wailers on the song "Africa Unite." Santa is a Jamaican reggae icon in his own right, but his collaboration with the Wailers on the Survival and Uprising albums demonstrated that he is one of the island's most in-demand musicians.

The Survival tour continued as the band travelled north into Canada before returning to the United States for a series of East Coast shows. Bob has been fighting a cold since the start of the Survival tour, despite his refusal to let anything stop him. Surprisingly, the cold would follow him throughout the tour. Stevie Wonder joined the Wailers on stage in Philadelphia on November 7 to perform "Get Up, Stand Up" and "Exodus." The Wailers then continued their journey to the West Coast across the Midwest. Stops in Michigan, Wisconsin, Illinois, and Minnesota were among the Midwest dates. The Wailers crossed the border once more for a show in Alberta, Canada, before continuing south along the western coast of the United States. The Wailers were greeted warmly in California, as they had been on prior tours. As the tour proceeded into the fall, they performed eight California concerts. Bob's health improved when he was in California. However, he appeared to be always exhausted and increasingly delegated his responsibilities, such as conducting interviews, to other members of the band. The group then drove through the southern half of the country, stopping only a few times. As the year came to a conclusion, the Survival tour came to an end. The band performed for the first time in Trinidad and Tobago before wrapping up the trip in Nassau at the Queen Elizabeth Sports Center.

In addition to the tour's excellent start, which included a headline appearance at the Reggae Sunsplash II concert and the Amandla success, the Survival tour included several other highlights. The November 25 performance in Santa Barbara, California, was recorded and then released on VHS (later upgraded to DVD). In addition, Rolling Stones guitarist Ron Wood made a special appearance during the November 30 event in Oakland, California. The tour concluded with a benefit concert for children in the Bahamas at the Queen Elizabeth Sports Center in Nassau, as part of the International Year of the Child. Bob contributed the earnings from his song "Children Playing in the Streets" to the charity that night. Bob wrote the song for four of his own children, Ziggy, Stephen, Sharon, and Cedella, who went on to form their own musical group, the Melody Makers, and recorded it as well.

Philosophically, the Survivor record was a piece of a greater puzzle that Bob was attempting to piece together. Bob laid the framework for his "call to action" for all black people with the album's sounds and lyrics. This message was delivered in three parts, as envisaged by the songwriter. The following album, Uprising, served as the second instalment of the trilogy. The third album, Confrontation, was released posthumously. Bob was deliberate in his delivery of his opinions on black action. The first step was to survive four centuries of oppression at the hands of white oppressors; the second was for the disenfranchised black population to band together and shake loose their shackles (literally or metaphorically); and the third was to relocate to a location where they would be free to live in peace (Africa). Even during the Survival tour, Bob was penning lyrics for new songs based on his intellectual journey -known bands, including Soul Syn-dicate. Since the 1970s, he has performed with nearly every prominent Jamaican popular group, including Jimmy Cliff, Black Uhuru, Burning Spear, Big Youth, Peter Tosh, Ini Kamoze, Big Mountain, and many others. During the Survival sessions, Santa sat in with the Wailers on the song "Africa Unite." Santa is a Jamaican reggae icon in his own right, but his collaboration with the Wailers on the Survival and Uprising albums demonstrated that he is one of the island's most in-demand musicians.

At least in part, Bob's idea became a reality. Because of the message in the song "Zimbabwe," African independence fighters used it as a rallying cry. Zimbabwe's Patriotic Front utilised the song to lift their spirits during their lengthy struggle for independence, and they saw Bob as a kindred soul from whom they might draw strength. The song articulated the reasons why many of the men were fighting in the first place, and it bonded them in a bond that would finally lead to triumph. This form of forecasting through music helped Bob's fame both during his life and after his death. Bob Marley swiftly became regarded as the universal voice of freedom, and he was quickly accepted as a figure to rally around by oppressed people everywhere (regardless of colour).

As the Survivor tour and 1979 came to an end, Bob and the Wailers began planning the band's schedule for the next year. They had already planned a band vacation to Africa, time in London, and album recording sessions. The release of Uprising, as planned, would result in a big tour. This served numerous functions. For starters, it was intended to bring the Wailers' music to a wider audience. Second, it fulfilled the objective of keeping Bob away from Jamaica for the 1980 general election. Third, it was to be the Wailers' first trip to Africa. The coordination of such a wide range of activities was a significant milestone. Bob renamed his company Tuff Gong International for these objectives, to reflect their ever-expanding worldview.

Because the Wailers toured in advance of the Upris-ing album's official June 10, 1980, release date in the United States, the band was already performing the new songs before the audience had heard them on the recording. The entourage of the Upris-ing tour left Kingston on January 1, 1980, and travelled first to London, then to Libreville, Gabon, in western Africa. Gabon is located on the African continent's west coast. Equatorial Guinea, Cameroon, the Republic of Congo, and the Gulf of Guinea border it. The Gabonese Republic, as it is officially known, gained independence from France in 1960. Since then, its president has been El Hadj Omar Bongo Ondimba (who has the distinction of being the country's longest-serving head of state). Because of its small population and enormous natural resources, the country is one of the most prosperous in the region.

The Wailers had been booked to perform for the president's birthday, and the enthusiasm in the band was evident. Bob was fulfilling one of his long-held dreams with this trip. The performance was also intended to introduce the Wailers' music to a previously unaware audience. The band had two gigs scheduled. Bob was ecstatic about performing in Africa; he had initially stated that he would cover the touring expenses personally as long as the Bongo family covered the Wailers appearance. He subsequently delegated the necessary arrangements with the oil-rich Bongo family to his manager, Don Taylor.

When the Wailers' touring unit, including opener Betty Wright, landed in Africa, they were shocked to hear that they would not be performing in front of the general audience. Instead, they were supposed to perform in a small tennis court for only 2,000 Gabonese elite. Although Bob was dissatisfied with the arrangement, he was pleased when young Gabonese people contacted him to discuss Rastafarianism during the group's two-week visit. The Wailers prepared to leave after performing the two contracted performances. This meant that the en-gagements had to be paid for. A disagreement occurred regarding the agreed-upon fee. Bob had agreed with Taylor that the Wailers would be paid $40,000 for their two appearances. Taylor was allegedly asking a price of $60,000, with the intention of pocketing the remaining $20,000 for himself. When a Bongo family representative learned that he was being blamed for the mistake, he went straight to Bob to clear things up. Bob reasoned with the individual and discovered Taylor's deception. Taylor had not only ruined the Wailers' otherwise positive African vacation, but he had also thrown doubt on Bob's reputation in the eyes of the Gabonese elite. Bob worked out everything with the Bongo family and their representative, and then he and Taylor got into a big fight.

Taylor allegedly blamed the entire incident on the Bongo family representative during their three-hour debate. Nonetheless, Bob was irritable. The specific details of the altercation are unknown, but the battle between Bob and Taylor resulted in Taylor ultimately admitting to mishandling Bob's money. He had a long-standing practice of receiving up to $15,000 in advance for each show and sending over only $5,000 to Bob and the band. Taylor also admitted to another form of theft from the Wailers. Bob would give Taylor money, sometimes as much as $50,000 at a time, to transfer to Family Man in Jamaica. Taylor subsequently sold this cash on the underground market for up to three times its face value. He then pocketed the illegal gains and only handed Family Man the original money. The Wailers' manager was evidently unwilling to provide this information, and while sources differ, it is conceivable that Bob asked that Taylor refund the money because of the severity of the betrayal. Of course, the shady band manager was unable to demonstrate his unlawful gains, claiming that he had lost all of his money gambling. Bob had little choice but to terminate Don Taylor and his band, who had been burnt yet again by the music industry.

The Taylor episode was only one of many examples of people in the music industry taking advantage of Bob. He struggled to earn adequate compensation for his music when he first began recording. This contributed to a general dislike for members of the music industry and exacerbated Bob's contempt for people in power. Bob has only one successful relationship with a music industry insider during his career. This fruitful collaboration was with Christopher Blackwell, the label owner of Island Records. Although Bob and Blackwell's relationship had its ups and downs, it was with Blackwell's assistance that Bob rose to international recognition. The Wailers returned to Jamaica from Africa and began work on new material. Bob had enough new material in his thoughts for these sessions to yield enough songs for two full-length albums. The first record made from these tapes was called Uprising. It was released in June 1980 and depicted Bob during one of his more belligerent periods. His lyrical substance was filled with biblical quotations, and his messages emphasised togetherness and salvation. The new material reflected his experiences in Africa, and the band's sound was heavier to represent Bob's attitude.

The Uprising album cover portrayed a victorious dreadlocked black man with his hands raised in the customary "V" for victory attitude. His hair was so long that it framed the album title, which was visible at his waist. Behind him was a picture of the sun rising over the top of a green mountain (perhaps depicting Jamaica's Blue Mountains). The album tracks have been hailed as some of Marley's best work. The album includes the songs "Coming in from the Cold," "Real Situation," "Bad Card," "We and Dem," "Work," "Zion Train," "Pimper's Paradise," "Could You Be Loved," "Forever Loving Jah," and "Redemp-tion Song." The album was jam-packed with solid gold singles. Uprising has become required listening for all reggae and Bob Marley fans in the years since its debut. Bob, the Barrett brothers as the rhythm section, the I-Threes, Junior Marvin, Tyrone Downie, Alvin "Seeco" Patterson, and Earl "Wya" Lindo all performed on the album. All of the tracks were recorded and mixed at Tuff Gong Studios in Kingston, Jamaica, and the 10-song testament to Bob's worldview has only become stronger with age.

The album's songs allude to Bob's past and raise an accusatory finger at people who mistreated or abused him. Bob's Rastafarianism could be heard on practically every tune. Most songs used biblical passages and paraphrases. Other themes that were prevalent included unity, love, and cooperation. Several biographers have speculated that Bob knew his health was failing and that he would not live much longer because of the harsh tone of his voice on this record. Several standout tunes on the CD had autobiographical lyrics. "Bad Card" was Bob's account of his interactions with Don Taylor. Taylor was the "bad card" that Bob got and with which he "made the wrong moves" in his business transactions. "Work" was another of Bob's calls to all downtrodden people to action. The song was written in the form of a reverse counting song, with Bob counting down from five. The countdown reflected the time remaining till the ultimate objective of liberty was attained. Bob concluded the song by saying that Jah's people can make it work.

On Uprising, Bob's usage of scriptural quotations and paraphrases in his lyrics reached new heights. Through the usage of the psalms, Bob invoked biblical sentiment, tale, and prophecy. This may be seen in the most famous song from the Uprising album, "Redemp-tion Song." Marley developed a series of visuals for this song. He first saw himself on a slave ship from the colonial era, but soon switched to biblical terminology from Psalm 88, describing being tossed into a bottomless pit. Bob also used text from Matthew 24:34 in the song to relate to killing prophets, and he allied himself with Joseph again by using language from Genesis 49:24. In the song, Bob was able to overcome these challenging situations with the assistance of the almighty Jah. Another intriguing aspect of the song was that it was Bob's only tune recorded without the assistance of a backup band. Bob was at his most intimate, singing with only an acoustic guitar for accompaniment. Although he didn't realise it at the time, "Redemption Song" was Bob's final song to be released.

Bob went to Miami for a few days after the sessions for Uprising were finished. He was fatigued and needed to recover, but he needed to sort out his management problem as he prepared for another lengthy Wailers tour. Simultaneously, he was acutely aware that his most recent album had fulfilled his record contract with Island. So, in addition to a new manager, he was about to lose his record deal. In Miami, Bob spoke with Danny Sims, who made it apparent that transferring labels and relocating to Polygram Records would be better for Bob's recording interests. Bob stayed with Blackwell's Island Records label. Polygram later purchased Island Records in a merger in 1989. Seagram purchased Polygram and absorbed it into the Universal Music Group in 1998.

In the midst of all of this turmoil, Bob decided to let off some steam by throwing himself a huge 35th birthday party. The audition was held on February 6, 1980, at 56 Hope Road. Bob surrounded himself with friends and family for the party, paying special attention to all of the children gathered in the Hope Road yard. Bob was frequently photographed engaging with youngsters throughout his life. Bob's generally stern demeanour softened in the presence of youngsters, as evidenced by these photographs. Bob noticed a difference in the music of his island home while celebrating his birthday in Jamaica. The reggae style he was driving was inspired by a new style known as "rub-a-dub." Papa Michigan and General Smiley were the most popular examples of this style in 1980. Michigan and Smiley, born Anthony Fairclough and Erroll Bennett, were two of the first dual DJ combinations to emerge in the Jamaican popular music industry. They gained rapid success after recording with Bob's former producer, Clement "Coxsone" Dodd. Their hit singles from this period were "Rub a Dub Style" and "Nice Up the Dance." They recognized Bob's star power and switched to his Tuff Gong Records label.

The rub-a-dub style, which was popular in the early 1980s, was distinguished by a quick tempo, extensive usage of the bass drum on beats two and four, and DJ toasting. Toasting was the Jamaican equivalent of rapping in New York, and it was accomplished by DJs delivering improvised lines over a prerecorded beat. The beats were derived from "dub plates," which were the B-sides of Jamaican singles that were released without the words. The emergence of rub-a-dub, Michigan and Smiley's switch to Tuff Gong, and the Jamaican ritual of toasting were just a few of the exciting changes in the Jamaican music industry in the early 1980s.

At the same time, Jamaica was devolving into politically motivated violence once more. While on the island, Bob was aware of the dangerous situation and kept to himself. His crew and family were usually around him, but he was wary of a recurrence of the 1976 assassination attempt. The Twelve Tribes of Israel Rastafarian fraternity helped to keep security around the reggae superstar. PNP and JLP conflicts during the run-up to the 1980 elections resulted in 750 deaths, and numerous polling stations did not open on election day owing to fear of violence. Bob retreated to Miami to strategize his next move after seeing that the Jamaican situation was spiralling out of control.

Bob learned while in Miami that Bucky Marshall had been shot and died at a block party in Brooklyn, New York, which made him apprehensive even in America. This unpleasant position was swiftly eased by delight when Bob and the band were invited to perform as part of the newly founded African republic of Zimbabwe's independence day celebrations. Bob was aware that his song "Zimbabwe" had become fairly popular in Africa, serving as a rallying cry for the continent's disenfranchised. He was, however, taken aback by the request to return to Africa and assist in the official declaration of the establishment of a new African nation. The leaders of the former Rhodesia realised that the political situation was too volatile to continue. Ian Smith formed a white minority party and declared unofficial independence from the British government in the mid-1960s. Smith faced off against Robert Mugabe's Zimbabwe African National Union (ZANU) and Joshua Nkomo's Zimbabwe African People's Union (ZAPU). This debate reached a peak in 1980, when a general election was held. Mugabe and ZANU won by a landslide, England severed all colonial relations with the country, and Rhodesia was renamed Zimbabwe.

Bob Marley and the Wailers were the proud headliners of the Independence Day celebrations, which commemorated Zimbabwe's official inauguration as a free African nation. Mugabe's general secretary, Edgar Tekere, phoned Bob to invite him to be one of the officiating dignitaries at the independence celebrations, citing the importance of Bob's music in energising Zimbabwean freedom fighters. After receiving the formal invitation to attend the celebration, Bob was approached by two African businessmen who invited him and the Wailers to play as part of the event. Bob was so moved by this that he agreed to have the Wailers perform and pledged to cover the band's travel fees himself. He was probably still thinking about the Don Taylor/Gabon debacle when he made these plans.

Although Bob and the band were overjoyed with their invitation to Zimbabwe, they were in serious trouble. The invitation had arrived on extremely short notice, and the band's absence of a manager had yet to be remedied. Regardless, Bob and the others persisted, and three days later they arrived at Salisbury Airport. The country's capital, previously known as Salisbury, was being renamed Harare. The Wailers were greeted at the airport by Joshua Nkomo, the leader of the ZAPU movement and Mugabe's minister of home affairs. Bob was astounded to be met by both Mugabe and Britain's Prince Charles. Mugabe was present to greet Bob and the band, and Prince Charles was the British representative who would drop his country's flag for the final time during the independence celebration. A Boeing 707 carrying equipment landed shortly after the Wailers were greeted in Salisbury/Harare. A 12-man road crew unpacked and set up 21 tons of Wailers gear, staging, lights, and a 25,000-watt amplification system with 20 foot tall speaker boxes. Bob Marley and the Wailers were gearing up for one of their most legendary performances in Jamaica. The band members regarded the concert appearance as the pinnacle of their musical careers.

The concert was scheduled for April 18, 1980, amid the celebrations of Rhodesia's independence. The Wailers expected they would be playing for the African masses once more, but were disappointed to hear that they would be performing soon after the independence celebration for an audience of dignitaries including Mugabe, Prince Charles, and India's Indira Gandhi. Bob Marley and the Wailers hit the stage at 8:30 p.m., directly following the inaugural raising of Zimbabwe's new national flag. Pandemonium erupted when the Wailers played their first notes in the Rufaro Stadium on the outskirts of the capital city. A large throng had gathered outside the venue's gates, and as they heard the band begin to perform, they rushed the gates. The crowd was too large to handle, and the national security force fired tear gas directly into the crush of gate crashers. While order was restored, Bob and the band were removed from the stage. The Wailers retook the stage when the throng was subdued. They were told they just had two minutes left in their allotted time, so they launched into a blistering rendition of "War." With their time running out, the band launched into "No More Trouble," followed by the show-stopping "Zim-babwe." The Wailers' show ended with everyone in the audience chanting along to the chorus of the nascent country's de facto national song.

Following their performance, the Wailers decided to perform again the following day. The Wailers performed in front of almost 100,000 people the day after Zimbabwe gained independence. The band performed a 90-minute concert of Wailers hits. However, Bob, who had been visibly frightened by the tear gas incident the day before, did not appear to be his typical self during the performance. Following the Zimbabwe gigs, the Wailers left Africa, and numerous members of the entourage remarked that Bob did not look to be in good health. His skin was pale, and he didn't appear well. Following their performance in Zimbabwe in April, the Wailers began their tour in support of their album Uprising in May. The tour was supposed to be the Wailers' most ambitious project to date. They were scheduled to perform in a number of new places, including Switzerland, Ireland, Scotland, and Italy. The tour schedule was tough, with six shows per week scheduled in different cities. Over the duration of the tour, the band performed in front of over a million people, a milestone few have matched since.

The tour began in Zurich, Switzerland, at the Hallenstadion. It was a first for the band, and it was well welcomed by the audience. The ensemble then proceeded to Germany for a performance at the Munich Horse Riding Stadium. On June 1, the ensemble opened for Fleetwood Mac as part of the Munich Festival. For the next two weeks, the tour alternated between Germany and France. The Westfalenstadion in Dortmund, Germany, hosted the show on June 12, which was broadcast on German television and videotaped for posterity. Bob was writing new music while on tour. The song "Slogans," for example, was not released until November 8, 2005, on the album Africa Unite: The Singles Collection. The song was a monument to the political lies and posturing that had repeatedly led to violent unrest in Jamaica.

The Wail-ers performed in Norway, Sweden, Denmark, Belgium, and Holland after departing Germany for the third time during the tour. They returned to France for two gigs before heading to Italy. Two gigs in Italy introduced the Wailers to a new audience before continuing on to Spain, France, Ireland, England, and Scotland. On June 27, the concert in Milan, Italy, was played in front of over 120,000 people squeezed into the sold-out San Siro Stadium. Surprisingly, this presentation is still regarded as the most popular music event ever organised in Italy. The Wailers went on the American portion of their tour after a month of European appearances. Bob returned to Miami for two months between the two halves of the tour after leaving Europe. Bob's financial affairs were in shambles, and things were only getting worse. Furthermore, following the fight with Taylor, Bob sued his ex-manager for a million dollars, and Taylor countersued. All of this was exacerbated when Bob heard that he would be unable to return to Jamaica to visit his children since the country had been rocked by violence in the run-up to the election. In Miami, Bob visited with Danny Sims, who warned him sharply about the dangers of returning to Jamaica. Sims feared Bob's arrival to the island at this time would be interpreted as an endorsement of the Manley PNP government, putting his life in danger once more. Despite the dire news, Sims did tell Bob that he had been working on a contract for the Wailers to transfer to Polygram Records, a transaction worth millions of dollars.

As the Wailers prepared for the American portion of their Uprising tour, there was growing concern and debate over Bob's health. The reggae icon appeared considerably slimmer than he had previously been, with drawn and haggard features. Members of the band blamed it on the band's hectic European tour schedule, citing their own diseases or ailments as a result of the tour.

The band began the American Uprising tour in Massachusetts in September 1980, then moved on to Rhode Island and New York. The American group the Commodores (Lionel Richie's first band) opened the New York gigs at Madison Square Garden. Bob appeared to be sick even after two months of rest. Bob, who was not one to discuss his health, brushed aside any attempts by band members to discuss how he was feeling. He only revealed his hand once, when he told his guitarist Al Anderson that his stomach and throat hurt. His voice was low and raspy, and whispers began to circulate regarding possible drug use (other than the massive amounts of ganja he usually smoked). Bob's health was clearly failing as the Wailers played their first American gigs of the Uprising tour. On September 18, the Wailers band moved into the Gramercy Hotel in New York, but Bob stayed at the Essex House, separate from the group. This solitude was not particularly concerning, as Bob occasionally remained at a location separate from the band to conduct interviews and band business. On September 19, Bob gave multiple radio interviews and attended the Jamaican Progressive League. He then proceeded to Madison Square Garden to get ready for the band's sound check.

The Wailers' sound check was pushed back because the Commodores' stage was still being built. This deferral eventually turned into an outright cancellation, much to Bob's chagrin. When the Wailers took the stage in front of 20,000 ecstatic fans that night, their road engineer had to arrange a respectable mix while the band was performing. The Wailers supported the Commodores with a two-night stint at Madison Square Garden. Bob was bedridden after the second show. The exertion of being on stage for the previous two nights had left him absolutely exhausted, and his health was once again called into doubt. Despite the fact that Bob was utterly exhausted, the tour proceeded on without him. Rita called to inquire if he wanted to go to an Ethiopian Orthodox Church, but he couldn't be lifted out of bed to go anywhere. However, Bob soon felt good enough to accept Alan "Skill" Cole's invitation to go for a jog in Central Park. Bob had a seizure while jogging through the park and shouted out to Cole. Cole took him back to the motel after he dropped into Cole's arms, unable to walk. Bob was able to move again after resting for a time, but he still didn't feel well.

CHAPTER 5

Home to Mount Zion

Bob napped for several hours after collapsing in Central Park. Rita quickly joined him, and the two of them tried to figure out what was wrong with him. Bob assuaged Rita's concerns by saying he was feeling better and simply wanted to rest. Rita agreed to meet Bob later at a local dance club, feeling confident that he would be fine. The club, Negril, was in Greenwich Village, and when Rita and the other I-Threes were there, they were told that Bob was too sick to join them. Bob's condition had once again deteriorated.

The following week, arrangements were made to go to Pittsburgh for the September 23 event at the Stanley Theater. Rita called Bob and asked him to meet her at the airport. Bob informed her he would see her in Pittsburgh since he had another interview in New York. There was no other interview, as it turned out. Concerned about his deteriorating health, Bob contacted his personal physician, Dr. Frazier, and scheduled an appointment. Bob agreed to a battery of X-rays and a brain scan. The test results halted Bob in his tracks. Bob was diagnosed with a huge malignant brain tumour by the doctor. Furthermore, the seizure he had in Central Park was a stroke. The doctor ordered Bob to cancel the remaining tour dates and to begin cancer treatment right now. The doctor's forecast that Bob had only two or three weeks to live was the worst of the bad news. Bob responded to the sad news in his normal stubborn fashion, saying that He was looking for a second opinion. He then planned to meet up with the tour in Pittsburgh. Rita greeted Bob as he arrived at the Wailers' hotel in Pittsburgh. Rita, recognizing the problem in Bob's expression, attempted to cancel the tour on the spot. However, sick or not, Bob was still the group's leader and would not accept a cancellation.

Bob Marley and the Wailers gave their final live performance on September 23, 1980. The play was performed at the Stanley Theater, a medium-sized yet intimate venue that has since been renamed the Benedum Center following extensive renovations. Bob took the stage the night of the performance and ripped through a fantastic set that included "Natural Mystic," "Positive Vibration," "Burnin' and Lootin'," "Them Belly Full," "Heathen," and "Running Away/Crazy Baldheads." The Barrett Brothers shifted the rhythms of the songs at a faster than usual speed during the Wailers' 90-minute set. Despite being terminally ill, Bob delivered his usual high-energy set, including "War/No More Trouble," "Zimbabwe," "Zion Train," "No Woman, No Cry," "Jamming," and "Exodus." At the conclusion of the standard set, the audience exploded in ovation. The Wailers then performed a series of encores. Bob didn't usually do four encores, but he stayed on stage as long as he could this night.

Bob performed the first encore alone, accompanied solely by his guitar. His rendition of "Redemption Song" was made more poignant by the fact that it was his final appearance. Following this solo performance, the remainder of the Wailers returned to the stage for the second encore, "Coming In from the Cold." This song's conclusion should have signalled the end of the concert. Bob, on the other hand, motioned for the band to stay on stage and tore into "Is This Love." The night ended with the Wailers' classic "Work." This song was written as an old-fashioned counting song (counting down instead of up), and its performance marked Bob's departure from the band. As he sang, "five days to go, working for the next day, four days to go now, working for the next day," the band members recognized that their leader was counting down the days till the band's demise. The concert was over, and Bob Marley and the Wailers exited the stage for the final time. Following the Pittsburgh performance, the remainder of the Uprising tour was cancelled, and the Wailers' touring machine was destroyed. The band and their entourage shifted their focus from performing to caring for and about Bob. Bob headed to his mother's house in Miami with Rita to plan his next step. Bob desired a second opinion, so he consented to more testing at Cedars of Lebanon Hospital. Cedars-Sinai recommended him to Memorial Sloan-Kettering Cancer Center in New York. Bob was tested by Sloan-Kettering scientists in early October. Bob hoped that the original diagnosis would be proven false. Instead, he rapidly discovered that his condition was far worse than had been claimed. He not only had a brain tumour, but he also had cancer in his lungs and stomach. With this more specific diagnosis, Bob was told that he only had four to five weeks to live and that he should organise his affairs. Bob began having radiation treatments to try to diminish the growth of the brain tumour in order to relieve the pressure generated by the tumour in his skull. Bob's illness was leaked to the media as a result of the Sloan-Kettering visit. Bob's cancer was disclosed on numerous New York radio stations on October 8, 1980. WLIB was the first station to broadcast Bob's health issues. The word travelled swiftly, and Bob's illness was soon known all over the world.

Bob relocated to New York to be closer to his treatment facility. He booked a room at the famous Wellington Hotel. The hotel's central position, only a few blocks south of Central Park, made it easy for Bob to get to his outpatient therapies and whatever else he wanted to do. Initially, Bob's radiation treatment was successful in managing his discomfort, and he gained stronger. In fact, Bob felt good enough to witness his pal Muhammad Ali's first rematch with Larry Holmes. The battle was advertised as the "Last Hurrah," and Ali fought hard, but he was defeated by a technical knockout by the much younger Holmes, who was in his prime and had been champion for nearly two years. Bob also saw Queen perform in New York as part of their tour in support of their 1980 album The Game. Bob felt good enough at times to return to his favourite sport, soccer. He and Cole tried to play, but Bob quickly discovered that he was too weak to run and could only sit on the sidelines and watch. Despite pushing himself and feeling better in general, Bob's health took a turn for the worst when he suffered another mild stroke. Bob was no longer able to stand without assistance as a result of the toll this put on his body, and he began to lose weight. When Bob's physicians realised this, they began administering chemotherapy. Unfortunately, Bob's long dreadlocks began to fall out as a result of this procedure. When this started, Bob asked for scissors to remove the rest of his locks and accepted the loss of his signature feature. Bob continued to lose weight as the chemotherapy progressed, and he took on an ashen aspect that seemed to indicate the end was nigh.

Cedella, realising her son was on the verge of death, began urging Bob to be baptised into the Ethiopian Orthodox church. Bob resisted at first when he expressed his devotion in Haile Selassie. Cedella, on the other hand, reminded Bob that she had been baptised while Bob was still in the womb. Bob continued his complaint, pointing out that his membership in the Twelve Tribes made him a natural adversary of Ethiopian Orthodox followers. Despite this, Bob agreed to be baptised and became a member of the Ethiopian Orthodox church on November 4, 1980. With this decision, Robert Nesta Marley was given the name Berhane Selassie. Bob's new moniker referred to the "Light of the Holy Trinity." Even as Bob's spirituality deepened, his health deteriorated. He was now immobile from the waist down as a result of the cancer and strokes, and he was still losing weight. It appeared that the treatment was hastening Bob's death.

Bob's physician, realising that the current course of action would not allow him to survive much longer, referred him to a German doctor called Josef Issels. Issels was well-known for his achievements in holistic cancer treatment. Despite being blacklisted by the American disease Society, his unique tactics could not cause Bob any more harm than the disease was already doing. Feeling as if they had nothing to lose, Bob, Cole, and Dr. Frazier hired Dr. Issels as Bob's last resort physician.

Bob and a small group of supporters headed to Bad Wiessee, Germany, in early November. They discovered Issels' clinic, Sunshine House, under the shadow of the Bavarian Alps. Bob's condition upon arrival was so bad that it was feared the voyage itself might kill him. When they arrived at Sunshine House, there was anticipation that Bob would only live for a few days. Issels began treating Bob right away. Gaining the trust of the cunning Rasta was a vital part of the treatment. Issels gradually acquired Bob's trust, and the doctor set about completing many tasks. He had to first stabilise

Bob's rapidly deteriorating condition before attempting to control the malignancy. The first step was to validate Bob's previous diagnosis. Issels began treating Bob's afflicted areas after determining the extent of the cancer in his head, lungs, and stomach. Issels' unconventional treatments included heat, blood transfusions, and THX injections. Hyperthermia was the process of artificially elevating the patient's temperature to levels that the body would not usually be able to withstand. Blood transfusions were utilised to cleanse the patient's body of the weak and overworked cells. Bob could not utilise THX in the United States because the medicine had not been approved for usage in the country. Surprisingly, some 30 years later, THX has yet to be demonstrated to have any objectively beneficial effect on cancer. However, under Issels' care and therapy, Bob's condition began to improve.

Surprisingly, Bob's health improved over the next few weeks. During this time, he and his mother shared a modest apartment at Sunshine House. Bob was able to walk small distances again as his condition improved. Two short walks to his treatment sessions were part of his everyday regimen. Dr. Issels proceeded to treat Bob with hyperthermia sessions, which involved blasting 180-degree beams of UV heat at his numerous tumours. The theory behind this treatment was that the high temperatures would weaken the cancer cells, allowing Bob's immune system to attack them more efficiently. The treatments were long, frequent, and terrible, but the brave Rasta bore it all in quiet.

Bob celebrated his 36th birthday three months into his therapy, much past the time when he was expected to die. Bob performed for many of the Wailers band members at a birthday celebration in Bad Wiessee on February 6, 1981. The Barrett brothers were the only members of the band who did not attend. Bob's supporters had expected to see their former leader close to death. Instead, they were greeted by Bob, who was in good spirits, in quite good health, and with part of his hair growing back. Bob became a part of the Tuff Gong International machine as a result of this gathering. Bob resumed oversight of his business through correspondence with his lawyer, Diane Jobson. This surge of activities seemed to boost Bob's strength to the point where he resumed modest exercise. Despite this progress, Jobson observed that Bob weighed just around 100 pounds at his birthday party.

While Bob's health was improving in early February, his mother noticed his condition worsening again towards the end of March. His strength gradually dwindled, as did his ability to walk without assistance. Cedella was unable to raise her son due to long periods of lying in bed. Bob's inability to eat or drink was another worrisome indicator. Ce-della realised then that Bob was not long for this earth. She was unable to improve her son's health, so she focused on increasing his spirits. Cedella spent time singing to Bob in this regard, reminding him of their pleasant moments together in the Jamaican hills and Kingston. Surprisingly, Dr. Issels chose to take a vacation at this critical juncture. Cedella was taken aback by the doctor's casual attitude toward her ailing son's health. In early April, Issels delegated responsibility for Cedella and Bob to his aides. Bob was now a mere shadow of his former self. His weight was assessed to be hardly more than 70 pounds, and he was unable to care for himself in any meaningful way. Jobson, Bob's lawyer, objected to the doctor's decision to leave at this time, but to no avail.

Bob's financial position exacerbated an already terrible scenario. It was well known that he lacked a will, and everyone expected that he wouldn't survive much longer. To make matters worse, members of the Wailers began making foreign calls pleading for their cut of the band's revenue. Bob's earnings, future royalties, and song licences would all transfer to Rita if he died without a will. Dr. Issels returned to Sunshine House late in April and decided to operate on Bob to ease the agony caused by the tumour in his stomach. Bob's Rastafarian beliefs were rekindled (in opposition to surgery's invasiveness). However, Bob's health was so bad that there was no other option. Bob's doctor told Ce-della and Jobson in early May that the most famous Wailer would most likely die within the next two weeks. Issels had given up on his own treatments to help Bob any more. In response to this news, it was determined that Bob should be returned to the Miami home he had purchased for his mother. Plans were made immediately to ensure that Bob would be able to make the journey. The little group rented a jet and returned to the United States. Cedella and Jobson checked Bob back into Cedars of Lebanon Hospital because they were unable to care for him. The staff was not directed to address Bob's now various ailments, but rather to keep him comfortable in his final days.

Bob survived the transatlantic flight but continued to deteriorate. Rita was called after his vital signs were irregular on May 11, 1981. She was advised that Bob had only a few hours to live and that she should be with him. Rita sat with Bob and sang hymns she knew he'd like. Soon, Bob's breathing grew laborious, and Rita summoned Cedella to be with her son. Bob's condition had improved by the time she arrived. Cedella and Rita prayed for Bob, who stated that he was feeling better. Bob bid goodbye to his kids Ziggy and Stephen at this brief protest. He also mentioned being thirsty. Cedella offered Bob a glass of water, which he drank all. Cedella assisted the staff in rolling Bob onto his side for an X-ray shortly before noon. Bob then fell asleep for a brief while. He requested his mum to come near to him as he awoke. He briefly lost consciousness as she did, and he silently drifted away. On March 11, 1981, at approximately 11:45 a.m., the blazing voice of international reggae sensation Robert Nesta Marley was silenced for the final time.

The following day, Bob was remembered in a service at his mother's Vista Lane home in Miami. Throughout the day, Bob's pals, including Sims, Taylor, Blackwell, and numerous musicians who had played with Bob, came through the house. Throughout the day, Bob's body was on exhibit. He was buried in a bronze casket that revealed his entire body from the waist up. His right hand held a Bible open to the Twenty-third Psalm, and his left hand held his favourite guitar. The inclusion of the 23rd Psalm was deliberate, as this biblical scripture proclaims that the Lord is the shepherd and that people who dwell in the house of the Lord need not dread harm. Bob's body was then brought to Jamaica for a state funeral. Bob's remains were returned to Jamaica on Tuesday, May 19, for a two-day state funeral organised by the prime minister's office. In 1981, Prime Minister Edward Seaga's office arranged for Bob to receive Jamaica's third highest honour, the Jamaican Order of Merit. Bob received this distinction and the accompanying medal, which reads, "He that does the truth comes into the light." Bob's eldest son, Ziggy, accepted the award on his behalf. With this, Bob was elevated to the position of Honourable. Robert Nesta Marley, O.M. Seaga also declared May 20 to be a national day of mourning, and Bob's body was laid to rest. The coffin was on display throughout the day for mourners to pay their respects.

Because of Bob's huge popularity, his body was on display in the National Arena for the entire day on Friday, May 20. This allowed even more mourners to view his remains, and according to accounts, up to 40,000 Jamaicans came through the arena's gates during the day. The cops used tear gas on the grieving as the throng expanded and became uncontrolled. During the chaos, Bob's body was guarded by Jamaican police and members of the Rastafarian organisation Twelve Tribes of Israel. Because of his conversion to the Ethiopian Orthodox Church, Bob's remains were carried to the church's headquarters on Maxfield Avenue the next day. Bob's body was given the traditional Ethiopian Orthodox funeral there. Bob's body was transported by mo-torcade from Maxfield Avenue to the National Arena, passing by his residence on Hope Road. A public service was held, with many of the Wailers performing. Tyrone Downie, who was too distraught to participate, was a noticeable omission. Bob's mother, his half-sister Pearl Livingston, and a family friend sang "Hail," a song composed by Bob's mother. The I-Threes then performed "Rastaman Chant" and "Natural Mystic" with the Wailers' backing.

Archbishop Yesuhaq presided over the public funeral service, which began at 11:00 a.m. Yesuhaq was the Ethiopian Orthodox priest who had baptised Bob the year before. Bob's immediate family, Governor-General Florizel Glasspole, and former Jamaican Prime Minister Michael Manley, Alan "Skill" Cole, attended the funeral. Yesuhaq assigned biblical scriptures to Glasspole, Manley, and Cole.

Cole repeated verses from Isa-iah and yelled at members of the Twelve Tribes who he thought were being ignored. The archbishop read from Matthew 5, and everyone in the congregation rose to their feet for the Lord's Prayer. Prime Minister Edward Seaga presented Bob's eulogy as the final speaker. Seaga's comments and thoughts were especially moving because he and Bob held opposing ideas on how to govern Jamaica. Regardless of their disagreements, Seaga said the following:

His message was a call to action against injustice and solace for the suffering. He stood there, performed there, and his message was heard everywhere. Today's funeral service is a native son's international right. He was born in the parish of St. Ann, nine miles from Alexandria, in a poor hamlet. As a child, he resided in the western section of Kingston and participated in the ghetto resistance. He absorbed the concept of survival as a child growing up in Kingston's west end. But it was his raw skill, unwavering discipline, and pure tenacity that propelled him from ghetto victim to top-ranking superstar in the third-world entertainment sector.

Following Seaga's eulogy, a military detail of six men dressed in white coats with black belts and black pants put Bob's casket into the open rear of a blue and white Chevrolet pickup truck. To protect the casket from the sun, a blue blanket was attached to the top of the truck's bed. As Bob set out on his final voyage to his ancestral home in Nine Mile, nyabin-ghi hand drummers accompanied him. The truck was briefly followed by a robed priest carrying incense. The long motorcade started its journey from Kingston to St. Ann's church. On the 55-mile journey, Bob's body passed thousands of Jamaicans who had gathered to say farewell to their national hero. Bob's body travelled through the Blue Mountains and was seen by a seemingly endless stream of people on the sides of the road.

When the convoy arrived at Nine Mile, it was met by yet another throng of well-wishers. Bob's body had arrived at its ultimate resting place five hours after leaving Kingston. A simple white mausoleum had been constructed on the grounds of Bob's paternal farm. Bob's remains were laid to rest in this single-chamber tomb near where he was born. Officials from the Twelve Tribes and the Ethiopian Orthodox Church blessed the grave. Bob's tomb was sealed three times in front of his family and many bystanders. The first seal was a red metal plate with a gold Star of David, the second was a bolted-on metal grating, and the third was a layer of free concrete patted into place with the bare hands of numerous Rastafarians. Bob was laid to rest with the pomp and fanfare usually reserved for leaders of state. It was estimated that over a hundred thousand people watched his motorcade throughout the burial and the travel across the island. Since his enshrinement, Bob's patriarchal home has become a pilgrimage site, with people travelling from all over the world to see the remains of the slain reggae warrior.

CHAPTER 6

The Legend and the Legacy

During his brief life, Bob got numerous big rewards. The 1976 Rolling Stone Magazine award for Band of the Year and the United Nations Peace Medal of the Third World in 1978 were two of the most notable. However, even in death, the reggae icon was lavished with adoration. These honours honour Bob's legacy and demonstrate the strength and influence of his musical approach. Bob was inducted into the Rock and Roll Hall of Fame in Cleveland, Ohio in 1994. With this, he became a member of a limited and exclusive group of American music superstars. The Rock and Roll Hall of Fame has only honoured 97 members since its inception in 1993, and Bob Marley is one of them.

Bob was also awarded with the 43rd Grammy Lifetime Achievement Award. He has a star on the Hollywood Walk of Fame, and Time magazine named his album Exodus the Album of the Century in 1999. The British Broadcasting Corporation (BBC) picked Bob's song "One Love" as their Millennium Song. Rolling Stone Magazine named him #11 on its list of the 100 Greatest Artists of All Time in 2004. In addition, the BBC has named him one of the greatest lyricists of all time. The Jamaican government yearly bestows the Bob Marley Culture Award, while the Caribbean Music Expo annually bestows the Bob Marley Lifetime Achievement Award. Bob has sold over 21.3 million albums since his death, which is possibly his finest award. To gain a better understanding of this amount, consider that such sales were not even recorded until 1991, when SoundScan became a trustworthy entity.

Bob received another special and rarely conferred honour after his death. Gibson began producing a limited edition Bob Marley Les Paul special guitar in 2002. Bob's favourite electric guitar for use on stage and in the studio was the Les Paul series. The iconic guitar maker joined forces with the legendary reggae artist as a memento of the label's appreciation for Bob's long affiliation with the Gibson brand. The Bob Marley Gibson Special was made exactly to the specifications of Bob's Les Paul, which is on exhibit at the Bob Marley Museum. Bob had made a few significant changes to his Les Paul, and Gibson replicated these features in the signature line guitar. The first batch of the Bob Marley Les Paul Special guitars was restricted to 200 pieces.

Bob's life beyond death has been filled with almost as much activity and interest as his earthly life. When Bob died, he left behind a massive library of recordings, but there were also many unpublished tracks that have continued to appear. Legend, Confrontation, Chances Are, Africa Unite: The Single Collection, Talkin' Blues, Songs of Freedom, Natural Mystic, the Legend Lives On: Bob Marley and the Wailers, and the Deluxe Edition re-releases were among the more significant posthumous releases.

Danny Simms released the nine-song album Chances Are in 1981. This album included previously unpublished material as well as updated versions of previously released material. Confrontation was released in 1983 by Tuff Gong International and Is-land Records. Bob had the idea for this record near the end of his life. He recorded the tracks during the Uprising sessions and was involved in every aspect of preparing this CD, except for selecting the individual songs featured and the order in which they appeared. Rita took over making these judgments.

Bob's career was reflected in the record. The album cover features the reggae superstar riding a white horse and conquering a dragon with a lance in the St. George pattern. The jacket's back included an artwork of the first combat between Ethiopians and Italians. This 1896 skirmish, known as the skirmish of Adowa, anticipated the warfare that eventually pushed Haile Selassie into exile. "Chant Down Babylon," "Buffalo Soldier," "Jump Nyabinghi," "Mix Up, Mix Up," "Give Thanks and Praises," "Blackman Redemption,"

"Trench Town," "Stiff Necked Fools," "I Know," and "Rastaman Live Up" were among the tracks on the album. The tracks are a wonderful representation of Bob's composing at the pinnacle of his powers.

Legend was the next major title published under Bob's name. The album was reissued in 1984 under the title The Best of Bob Marley. However, due to the vast volume of Bob's song output, 14 tracks were insufficient to achieve the stated aim. The CD, on the other hand, did a great job of giving a picture of Bob's production throughout his career. In true Wailers tradition, the remaining members planned a tour to promote the album. Downie and Marvin shared lead vocal duties, and Ziggy joined the tour for the Los Angeles gig. Legend lasted over two years on the American Top 200 Albums list and 129 weeks on the UK chart. Surprisingly, the record remained on Billboard's Top Pop Catalogue record chart for nearly 11 years. This album went on to become the best-selling reggae product of all time, earning ten platinum certifications. Legend had sold over 12 million copies as of 2006, and it is still selling well.

Bob Marley: Songs of Freedom, a four-CD boxed set released in 1992, was another significant release. The initial edition of this collection, which was officially licensed by Tuff Gong and Island Records, was restricted to one million copies. There was a second pressing in 1999 in a slightly different format, but this was still the definitive collection of Bob's songs, spanning his whole career. The album began with several of Bob's early singles and progressed to an acoustic version of "Redemption Song."

In November 2005, Africa Unite: The Singles Collection was released. Unlike many previous posthumous publications, this one had a clear purpose and was thoughtfully designed. The collection, which was released to commemorate Bob's 60th birthday, features a lot of his best work. The CD was unique in that it included songs throughout Bob's whole career, as well as two hip-hop remixes and a previously unheard track. The final three tracks on the album were the most important because they were not available anywhere else.

Will.i.am, of the American hip-hop group the Black Eyed Peas, was in charge of remixing "Africa Unite." Completed in December 2004, the song was given new life by a current producer/songwriter. The Black Eyed Peas added a louder beat presence, new instrumental textures, vocal echoes, and new lyrics spoken by Will himself. Overall, the remix was twice the length of the original song and received a hip-hop generation boost that carried it into the new millennium.

The other remix was more of a modern mashup. A mashup song is created by merging two existing songs in such a way that a third song that is a hybrid of the first two is created. Ashley Beedle, an English DJ, mashups Bob's fire-and-brimstone classic "Get Up, Stand Up" with Bob's son Damian's hit 2005 single "Welcome to Jamrock." The DJ reversed a record before dropping the beat from "Jamrock" into the combined version of the tune. Instead of sticking with Damian's lyrics, the DJ superimposed Bob's. The addition of the term "Jamrock" at the end of each sentence of Bob's lyrics was an extremely fascinating innovation. The presence of Peter Tosh was an added bonus. Tosh sung the second stanza in the original song, which was reproduced here (but just in recording: Tosh died in 1987). Bob's message was updated for the hip-hop generation once more with this song, but this time through the lens of his own son's song.

The album's only truly previously unreleased tune was titled "Slogans." The song was written in 1979 while Bob was in Miami. The song's initial recording was discovered in Cedella's residence and consisted of nothing more than vocals and a drum machine beat. Bob's sons Ziggy and Stephen created the rest of the tune from the raw cassette recording. They added musical lines to round out the texture, and the end result sounds very similar to other material created by their father. The lead guitar lines were supplied by the two

Mar-ley songs with the help of rock guitar icon Eric Clapton. The song's message was as relevant in 2005 as it was in 1979. Bob sang of his disdain for the Catholic Church and the Jamaican government's relentless propaganda. He was referring to the hollow promises made from the pulpit of the church and from the grandstand of a political rally.

The Deluxe Editions are another set of products that came out after Bob's death and are exceptional in quality and detail. In 2001, Island and Tuff Gong Records began re-publishing old Wailers work, releasing Catch a Fire, Exodus, Legend, Rastaman Vibra-tion, and Burnin'. These re-releases are one-of-a-kind in that they all include the original album material in remastered clarity by Dill Levenson. The second CD in each set varies from release to release. The second CD of Catch a Fire, issued in 2001, includes previously unreleased Jamaican versions of the songs from the first album. The first CD also includes recordings of "High Tide or Low Tide" and "All Day, All Night."

In 2001, the Exodus Deluxe Edition was also released. The first CD once again contains remastered versions of the original songs. Levenson, on the other hand, included five alternate songs and versions of "Roots," "Waiting in Vain," "Jamming," "Jamming (long version)," and "Exodus." The second CD featured a mix of studio and live cuts. Lee "Scratch" Perry recorded and produced the studio offerings. On disc two, there were two versions of "Punky Reggae Party," two cover versions of Curtis Mayfield's "Keep On Moving," and "Exodus." The live tracks were recorded on June 4, 1977, at the Rainbow Theater during the Exodus tour. There were songs like "The Heathen," "Crazy Baldhead," "War/No More Trouble," "Jamming," and "Exodus."

With the re-release of Ras-taman Vibration in 2002, the next Deluxe Edition was released. The first disc of the two-CD set once again includes remastered versions of the original album's tracks. Levenson supplemented this with eight extra tracks recorded in Kingston or

London at the same time as the original material. The second CD featured live performances from the Wailers' May 26, 1976, Roxy Theatre gig. The live recording, recorded during the Rastaman Vibration tour, was a remarkable tribute to the quality and potency that Bob had accomplished with this ensemble. On the second disc of this set, there were two versions of the song "Smile Jamaica," one labelled part one and the other part two.

Legend's Deluxe Edition was also released in 2002. The first CD contained digitally remastered music, and the second disc contained alternate versions of the original 16 songs. These versions were compiled from remixing sessions held between 1980 and 1984. Paul "Graucho" Smykle, Errol Brown, Alex Sadkin, and Eric "E.T." Thorngren are among the producers who re-mixed the songs on the second disc. The Legend Deluxe Edition, like the first release of this record, has been a consumer favourite.

In 2004, the most recent Deluxe Edition was released. The Burnin' instalment in this series included the restored tracks on the first CD, as well as five songs made during the original sessions but removed at the time. Because Burnin' was such an early album, two of the bonus tracks were written by members other than the original Wailers trio. Peter Tosh penned "No Sympathy" and Bunny Wailer wrote "Reincarnated Souls." A 12-song live set was included on the second disc. The live tracks were captured at the Leeds gig on November 23, 1973, using the Island mobile studio. All of the tracks on this disc were previously unreleased and represent the Wailers during their transitional period following the departure of Peter and Bunny.

Despite the fact that Bob has been dead for almost 25 years, posthumous releases by the artist continue. The reggae superstar's repertoire has grown multiple times since his death and shows no signs of stopping down. Imports, bootlegs, live shows, and many forms of compilations appear in waves. There were more than 12 full-length releases in Marley's name alone in 2006. Bob's content has totally saturated the market, and the monetization of the reggae legend is astounding.

The subject of money shifts to the administration of Bob's business interests following his death. As previously stated, Bob died intestate (without a will). This left his wife Rita in charge of the largest third-world music legacy and a multimillion-dollar estate. Years of acrimonious court disputes ensued over the rightful allocation of royalties, property, and ownership. Rita relocated the Tuff Gong Recording studios and production offices to 220 Marcus Garvey Drive, Kingston 11, following Bob's death. Tuff Gong International's headquarters remain at this location.

Rita's next project was to turn the house at 56 Hope Road into a museum and library where foreign visitors can receive guided tours of the grounds and house. Every year, thousands of people visit Bob's former home. The house's construction has remained unchanged since Bob's death, but various rooms have been modified to fit their specialised uses. The upper bedrooms have been transformed into gallery space, which includes a world map with colourful thumbtacks marking all of Bob's concert tour performance places. Ziggy's bedroom on the second floor has been turned into a makeshift business office and library. Books and newspaper articles regarding Bob and the Wailers are saved here and made available to researchers.

Bob's upstairs master bedroom is still in the exact state it was in when he last stayed there. Although Bob was a very prominent person, this room allows tour participants to see his more private side. Part of the original Tuff Gong recording studios may be found on the main floor of the property. The studios are still operational and are used on occasion. The kitchen is really interesting. The kitchen in the back of the house, which has been preserved since the mid-1970s, still has bullet holes in the walls from the assassination attempt in 1976.

The grounds surrounding 56 Hope Road are currently extremely populated. These grounds were utilised for parking and as a soccer field during Bob's lifetime. The grounds are now dotted with a number of tourist attractions. Rita's Queen of Sheba Restaurant, located at the edge of the yard, serves traditional Italian cuisine and fruit cocktails. Behind the house, where there was once practice space, is now a newer structure that houses the Bob Marley Theatre. Another relatively recent building along the site holds the Things from Africa Boutique.

Rita suffered from a lack of experience when handling Bob's estate, in addition to managing the property at 56 Hope Road. Almost every aspect of Bob's massive empire's management was fraught with difficulty. Money was syphoned, relationships with Wailers band members were strained, and a lot of time and money was spent trying to figure out what was going on. One such blunder occurred in 1986, when the remaining members of the Wailers band were practically compelled to sign away their rights to future income in exchange for a fixed price. The sums ended up being cents on the dollar in the future, but they were immediate payoffs.

Rita's stewardship of the Marley estate deteriorated once more in 1987. Rita, her accountant Martin Zolt, and her attorney David Steinberg were all charged with fraud. Rumours circulated in Jamaica that Rita was hiding money in the Cayman Islands, dividing Bob's estate into taxable and untaxed income. Rita was removed from management at this point and replaced with a court-appointed bank administrator. This caused numerous issues for the Marley family, as their collective assets were blocked and Cedella's Miami home was temporarily seized.

Much of the early proceedings of Rita, Zolt, and Steinberg's trial are hazy. The trio, on the other hand, was found to be guilty of fraud, breach of fiduciary duty, and violations of the Racketeer Influenced and Corrupt Organizations Act (RICO). Because Bob died intestate, Jamaican law rendered Rita liable for 10% of his estate outright, plus

45% held as a life interest. Each of Bob's 11 children was entitled to an equal share of the remaining 45 percent outright, as well as a remainder interest in Rita's 45 percent life estate. During the initial proceedings, it was also discovered that from 1981 to 1986, persons in charge of Bob's estate engaged in multiple scams that allegedly moved overseas music assets and royalty money away from Bob's estate and into accounts kept outside the estate. Rita, Zolt, and Steinberg objected, claiming that the diverted monies were used to form new corporations in order to reduce tax burden and leave more money for Bob's beneficiaries. Lawyers for the state cited at least four schemes and supplied signed documents demonstrating the three defendants' collaboration. In summary, Rita and her representatives failed to record the majority of the royalties earned by Bob's music.

For a period, Bob's musical legacy was eclipsed by lawsuits, deception, and instability. As a result of these legal manoeuvrings, the Jamaican government decided to sell the Bob Marley estate as a whole. Bob's longtime buddy and record industry owner, Chris Blackwell, purchased the estate for the pittance of $8.6 million. Despite objections from members of Bob's own family, Blackwell's company, Island Logic Inc., won the auction for Bob's estate. Blackwell paid $8.6 million for the rights to all of Bob's songs, re-recordings, and future royalties. In 1989, Blackwell sold the rights to Bob's discography to the German record business Polygram. In 1998, Polygram was acquired by Seagrams, and the new music collective was dubbed the Universal Music Group. As a result, Bob's music changed hands yet again.

Bob's impact endured despite all of the legal hurdles and difficulties in determining ownership. Despite the loss of the initial licensing, Bob's family has remained financially secure because they control all other areas of his output. Furthermore, unreleased material was not covered by the initial court agreement, and as a result of the surfacing of many extra versions and studio outtakes, most of Bob's music is now controlled by his family. Regardless of who owns Bob's music, his ultimate legacy, in his own words, was in his children.

CHAPTER 7

The marley family

The Marley family's two living matriarchs are the primary protectors of the family legacy. Even more than 25 years after Bob's death, his mother Cedella and wife Rita continue to carry on his work. Although Cedella was not always involved in Bob's work during his lifetime, she has become increasingly involved since his death. She is the oldest member of the Marley family and the guardian of his legacy. Cedella Marley Booker (born July 23, 1926) still lives in the Miami, Florida home that Bob purchased for her. She serves as the family's official matriarch and is still active in many of the family's business. She has cared for both the children Bob had with Rita and his children born outside of the marriage. His mother has recorded two CDs of her own music as part of her efforts to preserve her son's legacy. Awake Zion was released on the RIOR label in 1991, with the help of Bob's old bass player, Aston "Family Man" Barrett. The following year, she released her second album, Smilin' Island Song.

Cedella has also published a number of novels about her son's life. She wrote Bob Marley: An Intimate Portrait by His Mother, as well as Bob Marley My Son. Furthermore, mother "Ciddy" has travelled extensively, speaking about the significance of her renowned son and singing her own songs. Her tours have carried her across the United States, much of Western Europe, into Africa, around Mexico, and all the way through the Caribbean. She has just begun making handcrafted dolls, which are sold on numerous websites. Rita Marley, born Alpharita Anderson in Cuba on July 25, 1946, was the Marley family's other main leader. Rita's legal issues grew after Bob's death, and she lost control of the Marley family money. Despite this first setback, Rita was able to sustain herself and her family and develop a new wealth. Rita's contribution to Bob's legacy included the publication of her own music. She released the album Who Feels It Knows It in 1981, Harambe in 1988, and We Must Carry On in 1988. Rita began her musical career as the leader of her own band, and after years of singing backup to Bob, she returned to front woman form.

Rita released a new album series in the 1990s. These records were released on the Shanachie label. Beauty of God, Good Girls Cult, and One Draw were among them. These were followed in the new millennium by Sings Bob Marley... and Friends, Play Play, Sunshine After Rain, and Gifted Fourteen Carnation. Rita also published a book on her life with Bob, which offers a unique perspective on a woman dealing in a male-dominated scene. No Woman, No Cry: My Life with Bob Marley was written in collaboration with Hettie Jones. Rita has recently stayed involved in the music industry, owing largely to the efforts of her several children. She is working to preserve and safeguard her husband's legacy, and she attends annual worldwide birthday celebration performances in his honour. Rita has also established the Rita Marley Foundation to deliver much needed supplies and infrastructure improvements to Africa's underprivileged areas. The group's major purpose is to offer safe drinking water to thousands of Africans struggling for survival.

Rita declared her plan to have Bob's body taken from the mausoleum at Nine Mile and reburied in his spiritual home in Ethiopia in January 2005. This announcement came as part of Bob's 60th birthday celebration, which lasted a month. Ethiopian religious and government officials supported the action. Rita claimed at the time that it was part of Bob's mission to return to Africa, and that the movement of his casket would fulfil the late reggae legend's wishes. Rita recommended reburying Bob's body in Shashamane, about 155 kilometres south of Addis Ababa. On his first journey to Africa, Bob had visited this Rastafarian colony. Many Jamaicans were outraged when Rita made her revelation. The Bob Marley Foundation promptly denied Rita's accusations, stating that there were no intentions to relocate Bob. In fact, the news of a prospective reburial sparked such a strong backlash that Rita was obliged to retract her earlier statement. Rita initially stated that no choice had been taken, but she eventually stated that Bob's remains would remain in Nine Mile. The uproar over the prospective relocation sparked increased interest in all things Marley in the run-up to his 60th birthday celebration, but there was fear that this enthusiasm was more negative than positive. Regardless of any blunders, Rita remains the Marley family's focal point. She is still very involved in the management of the Marley legacy and has taken on the role of mother to all of Bob's children, despite Bob's adulterous affairs.

Bob's love for children was constant throughout his life. He included not only his own children, but all children around the world. With this in mind, Bob's most lasting legacy may be his 11 children. Bob's opinions on the subject were conveyed in his declaration that he wanted as many children as there were shells on the beach. Regardless of moral rules, Bob fathered three children with Rita and adopted two of her other children. Bob adopted Rita's daughter Sharon, whose biological father was an unidentified man with whom Rita had her daughter prior to meeting Bob. Bob was also unlikely to have fathered Rita's daughter Stephanie. It is widely assumed that Stephanie's father was a Rasta named Ital. Bob treated these children as if they were his own, regardless of their dads.

Bob had multiple high-profile affairs during their marriage. Rita later embraced many of these affairs' offspring into the larger Marley family unit. Damian, Rohan, Robbie, Karen, Julian, Ky-Mani, and Makeda Jahnesta were some of Bob's other children. Each child had a distinct role in Bob's life, and numerous of his children, both from his marriage to Rita and from other relationships, continue Bob's musical legacy.

Although Bob was not the biological father of Sharon (born Sharon Marley Prendergrass), he raised her as a daughter his entire life. When he and Rita married, he adopted her and lavished her with attention. Sharon, sometimes referred to as Bob's "favourite," has dedicated her life to advancing many areas of Bob's vision. Bob was Sharon's father from the age of 18 months, and like any good father, he tried to guide her in her life's objectives. The Marley household was constantly filled with music when she was growing up. Sharon became increasingly aware of life in the music industry as Bob's celebrity expanded. Her father, on the other hand, warned her against pursuing music as a career since he understood firsthand how difficult it is.

Even with her father's advice ringing in her ears, Sharon has worked in the music industry as an adult. As a member of Bob Marley's children's band, the Melody Makers, she has helped to preserve Bob's musical legacy. She is the current curator of the Bob Marley Museum in Kingston, Jamaica, and she has pursued an acting career, appearing in the Denzel Washington/Robert Townshend film The Mighty Quinn. Sharon's professional activities also include her work with the Caribbean company Ghetto Youths International and her efforts to open a daycare training centre in Jamaica. The centre would be the first of its kind on the island, and it would reflect Bob's passion in child care.

Cedella, after Bob's mother, was the name of the first child born from Bob and Rita's marriage. Cedella was born in Kingston in August 1967, coinciding with the release of the Wailers track. "Nice Time." As a result, she was given the song's title as a moniker. She grew up in a fairly traditional household, attending public schools. Bob, like Sharon, wanted Cedella to be a doctor or a lawyer, but she chose to follow in her father's footsteps and pursue a career in music.

Cedella was instrumental in the formation of the Marley children's ensemble, the Melody Makers. She is well-known for her lovely singing voice and is also a skilled dancer. Cedella developed a separate group named the Marley Girls in addition to the Melody Makers. Her professional involvement with Bob's legacy stems from her position as CEO of Tuff Gong International. Cedella finds time to be engaged in raising her own set of Marley children in addition to recording, performing, and managing Bob's record label. Cedella, known for her toughness, works tirelessly to preserve and expand her father's legacy.

David, Sharon and Cedella's next younger sibling, was born on October 17, 1968. Although David was his given name, he was quickly called Ziggy and has gone by that name ever since. Ziggy was admonished again not to follow in his father's musical footsteps as a child, but he was bitten by the musical bug. He grew up listening to his father's music, as well as that of great American artists like Stevie Wonder.

Insiders in the music industry believe Ziggy is the inevitable heir to his father's musical reign. He has many of his father's facial traits, as well as Bob's voice. He was also able to see and participate in aspects of Bob's musical trip due to his age. Ziggy was in Zimbabwe with his father for a concert commemorating the country's independence. After his father died, he became the de facto head of the family. As a result, he was awarded Bob's Order of Merit on behalf of his father.

Ziggy was the Melody Makers' musical director as a musician. This became obvious when the band was renamed Ziggy Marley and the Melody Makers. Ziggy has gone on his own musical voyage after his father's death. Unlike many of the other Marley children, he has pursued a solo career after working with the Melody Makers on seven studio albums (and several best hits collections).

The Melody Makers are the most well-known Marley children's musical group. Sharon, Cedella, Ziggy, and Stephen make up the group. In 1979, the members of the group recorded a song written by Bob for and about them called "Children Playing in the Streets." However, the group was established unofficially in 1981 to sing at Bob's burial. The Melody Makers have regularly released marketable reggae music that honours their father's legacy since their inception. Although the group's musical output varies from pop to more serious roots-sounding pieces, the group's output as a whole has been a testament to its members' musical history.

The Melody Makers have released various albums over the span of several decades. They've also toured overseas and performed as part of their father's Reggae Sunsplash concert series. Their first album, Play the Game Right, was released in the mid-1980s. Hey World! was their second album, released in 1986. This was followed by 1988's One Bright Day and 1989's Conscious Party. The Melody Makers' style of reggae music at the time was inspired by their father's material, but did not sound much like it. The Melody Makers' products, on the other hand, were economically viable and of sufficient quality that they were in demand as singers and songwriters.

The group's albums continued to be released throughout the 1990s. Jahmekya was released in 1991, and Fallen Is Babylon was released in 1997. Spirit of Music, the group's 1999 album, was hailed as a return to conscious reggae roots. The Melody Makers have continued to forward their father's, and by extension reggae music's, goal of presenting conscious music to the masses via their many releases. Surprisingly, after Bob's death, the dominant form of Jamaican popular music shifted away from roots reggae and toward dancehall. Dancehall has far more in common with American hip-hop than with conscious reggae's social or political issues. Instead of following in their father's footsteps, the Melody Makers continued to forge their own path with their music.

Ziggy grew as a vocalist and songwriter in this environment. Taking a page from his father's book of ambition, Ziggy went about writing music for a global audience. He has reached that audience and achieved an American Top 40 hit as proof of his achievement. To say Ziggy got off to a good start is to state the obvious. With his father's good features and attractive voice, he was the ideal front man for the Melody Makers, but he ended up fronting an internationally viable group at the age of 17. One might imagine that following in Bob's footsteps made Ziggy's entry into the music industry simple. On the contrary, his father had left him with enormously wide shoes to fill, and Ziggy's youthful songwriting abilities paled in comparison to Bob's mature work.

Ziggy allowed his music to move further into popular mainstream circles early on in order to build out his own niche. The roots reggae core was outraged, but it was assumed that the young Marley was merely establishing his own voice and freeing himself from the huge strain of his father's musical heritage. Another issue in Ziggy's life at the time was EMI's (the Melody Makers' record company) strong desire to promote Ziggy as a solo performer rather than as the leader of a group of his siblings. Because of this conflict, the band decided to sign with Virgin Records.

Their most popular material to date comes from the transfer to Virgin. The tracks on Conscious Party were a huge hit for the band. This release, which was produced with the help of Talking Heads members Chris Frantz and Tina Weymouth, was both economically and critically successful. The album reached number 39 on the American popular music charts, proving that the Melody Makers were not simply riding on the coattails of their renowned father.

Ziggy and the Melody Makers' 1989 follow-up to Conscious Party, One Bright Day, was another huge success. The album debuted in the top 20 in the United States, proving that the previous album was not a fluke. Both of these late-1980s releases received Grammy nominations for Best Reggae Album of the Year. With the publication of the Jahmekya album in the early 1990s, the band's success continued. The album sold well and reached the Top 20; nevertheless, unlike the previous two albums, it lacked radio-friendly singles. Joy and Blues, Stephen's 1993 follow-up album, had some dancehall-style tunes. The album was a flop, and it signified the band's exit from Virgin Records and relocation to Elektra Records.

The group released Free Like We Want 2 B for Elektra in 1995. With this, Ziggy and the Melody Makers appeared to have regained part of their original form. Fallen Is Babylon garnered the trio another Grammy Award in 1997, demonstrating Ziggy's songwriting prowess. Ziggy developed as a soloist from the ensemble during the course of these latter releases. The Melody Makers are still a band in name, but Ziggy has started working on solo projects.

Ziggy was becoming a prominent political voice in addition to his solo activities. He was awarded a United Nations Goodwill Youth Ambassador and has spoken publicly against injustice, poverty, and the Third World. In addition, he founded his own record label, Ghetto Youths United (Ghetto Youth Crew), to nurture the creativity of the next generation of reggae performers. His charitable activity is highly known, and he has been involved in United Resources Giving Enlightenment (URGE), a community service organisation in Jamaica.

Ziggy continued to develop as a solo performer and leader of the next generation of Jamaican music in the new millennium. On April 15, 2003, he released Dragonfly, his first official solo album. Ziggy is depicted on the record cover with dreadlocks to his waist and a dragonfly on a yellow background. He was recognized as the writer and singer for all 11 songs on the album, which was a moderate hit. Ziggy followed this up with a second solo album, Love Is My Religion, in 2006.

Ziggy has had a diverse career in the entertainment sector in addition to music. In 2004, he played a Rasta jellyfish in the film Shark Tale, and he and Sean Paul collaborated on a new version of his father's song "Three Little Birds" for the soundtrack. Ziggy also sung the theme song for the PBS show Arthur and is developing as a soloist. As he grows into a leadership role in the international reggae community, his voice becomes more and more like his father's.

Ziggy, like Bob, has fathered a large number of children. Ziggy has three children with his long-term partner Lorraine Bogle: Daniel (a son), Justice (a daughter), and Zouri (a daughter). Ziggy is currently married to Orly Agai, with whom he has five children. Their daughter Judah Victoria was born on April 7, 2005, and their son Gideon Robert Nesta Marley was born on January 5, 2007. While pursuing his own career, humanitarian and philanthropic pursuits, and family interests, Ziggy recalls his father's words: "every man has to stand up for his rights."

Stephen, Bob's second son, was the next Marley kid, born on April 20, 1972. Rita and Cedella were residing in Wilmington, Delaware when Stephen was born. Stephen, the Melody Mak-ers' youngest member, has achieved success as a singer, DJ, writer, and producer. His first recordings were recorded when he was six years old, when he assisted in the recording of "Children Playing in the Streets." The song was recorded for charitable purposes, and the single's revenues were donated to the United Nations in support of the International Year of the Child. Stephen also danced and performed in Bob's live shows, spending time on stage. In addition to spending his childhood on stage with his father, Stephen began learning the acoustic guitar at the age of seven.

Stephen has been involved in music and a professional musician for the most of his life as a result of his early exposure to the art form. In addition to playing, he is a founding member of the record company Ghetto Youths United. As a producer, Stephen has created several well-known remixes of his father's work, collaborating with prominent living singers such as Lauryn Hill (one of the Fugees' three members). His collaboration with Hill resulted in the Melody Makers performing alongside the Fugees at the 1997 Grammy Awards Show in New York City.

Stephen's production career began in 1996, when he produced tunes for his brothers Damian and Julian's albums. Stephen's production work has also allowed him to experiment with a wide range of musical styles. He's experimented with reggae, hip-hop, and rhythm and blues. Work with hip-hop artists such as Krayzie Bones (of Bone Thugs-N-Harmony), Eve (of the Ruff Ryders), and Erykah Badu has strengthened his credibility and linked his father's heritage to current musical forms.

He worked as a producer on his brother Damian's 2001 album Halfway Tree. The album was a smash hit, earning a Grammy for Best Reggae Album of the Year. His rendition of Stevie Wonder's Bob Marley tribute song "Master Blaster" was so good that it was included on Wonder's 2005 tribute album, Conception. Stephen has not been as prolific as some of his siblings as a songwriter. He started working on an album in 2002, but it was pushed back due to his work with the Ghetto Youths International production business. The album, titled Got Music?, was supposed to be released in 2006. Despite the fact that the tracks were finished, Stephen chose not to release the album. Some speculated that the album was delayed to prevent conflict with other Marley family releases. Mind Control, Stephen's debut full-length album, was released in 2007. He is now streaming the title track from the album on his Myspace page, and expectations are high for a successful, long-awaited release.

Despite being in his mid-thirties, Stephen has already had an almost three-decade career in music. As a result, the release of his CD has sparked considerable attention. The CD is a unique and nameless hybrid of reggae, rock, rhythm and blues, nyabinghi, flamenco, and hip-hop. The Mind Control album includes cameos by Ben Harper, Mos Def, Damian Marley, Maya Azucena and Illestr8, Spragga Benz, and Mr. Cheeks, as is usual in current American hip-hop.

Stephen has done wonders for Bob's musical legacy by bringing his father's songs to a whole new audience during the course of his career. Stephen is a five-time Grammy winner in his own right and is only getting started in what looks to be a long and profitable career. Stephen's combative attitude and disdain for shady political practices are evident in his lyrics, and he consistently conveys his father's message. Stephen participated in two American tours in 2006 to help preserve the heritage. The critically praised Bob Marley Roots, Rock Reggae Festival, which also featured his brother Ziggy, was the most memorable. On this tour, Stephen shared the stage with Bunny Wailer, one of his father's oldest friends and one-third of the original Wailers vocal three.

Stephen, like the majority of the Marley offspring, has his own children. He was previously married to Kertie DaCosta, with whom he had a son, Jeremiah, and a daughter, Sasha. He also had four more children from previous partnerships. His other children include three sons, Joseph, Stephan, and Yohan, as well as a daughter named Summer. Stephen is currently married to fashion designer and singer Kristina Marawski, with whom he has a daughter named Zipporah.

Stephanie, another Marley daughter, was born in 1974. There are some different reports about her ancestry. Some say Bob was her father, while others say Ital, a local Rasta, was her father. Stephanie's father was most likely Bob, according to Rita in her book No Woman, No Cry: My Life with Bob Marley. However, Rita and Bob were not getting along at the moment, and Rita had begun a relationship with a local Rasta named Tacky. Tacky, a local Rasta, was actually Jamaican soccer legend Owen Stewart. Rita was extremely cautious not to say that she and Tacky had a sexual relationship in her book, but it was implied.

Stephanie was born on August 17, 1974, regardless of who her biological father was, and Bob was her father for all intents and purposes. She was raised in Kingston and attended Jamaican basic and high institutions. She relocated to England and finished her A-levels in psychology and social studies in London. Stephanie then went on to study psychology at the University of Western Ontario in Canada. She received her bachelor's degree with honours and was involved with local children's groups during her studies. She was especially attentive to youngsters with special needs.

Stephanie returned to Jamaica after graduation and joined the family company. She rose through the ranks to become the managing director of the Bob Marley Foundation, Bob Marley Museum, Tuff Gong International, Tuff Gong Recordings, URGE, and the Rita Marley Foundation. Stephanie's work also helped to preserve her father's legacy. Stephanie is now directing the construction of the first Marley Resort and Spa in Nassau, Bahamas. Stephanie, who is more business-oriented, promotes events through Tuff Gong Productions and organises the annual Reggae All-Star Concert in Nassau. Stephanie also has four sons, all of which are boys.

Bob fathered the remainder of the Marley children in relationships other than his marriage. Each child had a different mother; but, following Bob's death, Rita has taken on the role of mother figure for the majority of Bob's children. Bob had seven extramarital encounters with women who bore him children. Some of his partnerships were well-publicised, such as his "Beauty and the Beast" marriage to Cindy Shakespeare. Other child-producing meetings, such as those with Evette Morris (Crichton) and Janet Hunt (Dunn), were brief and little documented. The children born from these couplings have been equally responsible for preserving their father's legacy, and many of them have made significant contributions to the music industry.

In the early 1970s, Bob met Janet Hunt (or possibly Dunn). Janet was a club dancer who drew Bob's attention. Little is known about their encounter; but, as a result of it, Janet gave birth to Bob's son Rohan. Rohan Anthony Marley was born in May 1972, and his mother gave him to Bob and Rita when he was four years old. Rohan officially became a Marley at this point. He attended the same high school as Ziggy and Stephen. Unlike his brothers, Rohan was more interested in athletics than music. The Marley family had difficulty keeping track of this outgoing adolescent, so he was sent to live with Bob's mother in Miami.

Cedella adopted Rohan, who thrived in her care. He graduated from Miami Palmetto Senior High School in 1991 and went on to play linebacker for the University of Miami's football team. Rohan then played for the Ottowa Rough Riders of the Canadian Football League for a short time. Rohan opted to slow down and refocus his efforts after his time playing football.

Rohan recently married Lauryn Hill and started working for the Marley family enterprises. Rohan, for his part, works with the Tuff Gong Clothing Company to keep Bob's memory alive. Rohan designs clothing that is designed to be universally appealing, much like his father's music. Rohan spends time with his own set of Bob's grandchildren in addition to his work with the apparel line. He and Lauryn have four children: sons Zion David, Joshua, and John, and a daughter called Selah Louise.

Bob's next child was the result of his affair with Pat Wil-liams. Williams was a Trench Town woman with little information about her. In reality, her first name is unclear: some claim Pat, while others suggest Lucille. The account of her brief relationship with Bob, on the other hand, was recorded in his song "Midnight Ravers." The scene was detailed in the evening news and in the song itself. Bob had been standing naked in the moonlight outside the house at 56 Hope Road. Williams approached him at the moment and seduced him. Bob awoke the next day and scribbled the lyrics to "Midnight Ravers" on a Kingston phone book. This meeting produced Robert Nesta Marley II, also known as Robbie.

Rita was responsible for Robbie, as well as many of the other children born as a result of Bob's business dealings. Robbie attended the University College of the West Indies, where he studied computer graphics, with the help of Rita and the Marley family. Robbie has been active in a variety of activities since then. Vintage Marley is his apparel boutique in Miami, Florida. He began riding motorcycles and has since become an accomplished stunt rider. This led to a cameo appearance in the 2003 film 2 Fast 2 Furious. He also runs a motorcycle riding group named the Miami Warriors. Robbie's four children, Kaya, Ekitai, and twins Regal and Robert, add to the Marley family tree.

Bob's affair with Janet Bowen resulted in the birth of another Marley child. Again, there are few specifics about Janet, but she is referred to as "Janet in England" in various texts. In 1973, Janet gave birth to a daughter called Karen. Janet and Karen are both steeped in mystery, as neither has sought the limelight. Janet lived in Harbor View, St. Andrews, Jamaica, with her great-grandmother. She grew up and attended school here. Her connection with the Marleys has been minimal. Karen was a frequent visitor to the Marley home in Kingston, but she did not fit in with the other kids. When Bob's health began to decline, he asked Rita to care for Karen, and she sent her to school with Stephanie. Karen's current existence is unknown because she has chosen to live her life away from the light and scrutiny of the public eye.

Lucy Pounder was a Barbadian resident who, while little is known about her time with Bob, did give birth to Julian Marley on June 4, 1975. Julian was born in London and raised there, but he frequently visited Rita and the other Marley children in Jamaica and Miami. Julian began studying bass, drums, and keyboard at a young age, following in the footsteps of his musical family. As a child, he was also a talented songwriter. At the age of five, he released his first single, a cover of his father's song "Slave Driver," which was recorded at the Marley family's Tuff Gong Studios in Kingston. This was only the beginning of a busy and profitable career.

Julian's musical strength was fully realised in the 1990s. He founded his own band, the Uprising band, and released the album Lion in the Morning in 1996. Julian was credited with authoring or co-writing all of the songs on the critically acclaimed album. Julian, following in his father's footsteps, toured in support of the album and performed internationally as a soloist backed by the Uprising band and as a member of Ghetto Youths International. He learned a lot from his brothers Stephen and Damian while he was a member of Ghetto Youths. Julian, together with Damian, opened for Ziggy Marley and the Melody Makers on their 1995 tour, and he was a featured musician on the 1999 Lollapalooza Festival Tour (quite a coup given that this was a rock-oriented tour).

Julian was ready for the next challenge when the millennium began. Julian collaborated with his Marley brothers to create the platinum-selling Chant Down Babylon CD, which featured contemporary singers alongside Bob Marley from beyond the dead. He also contributed to the Stevie Wonder tribute song "Master Blaster" with his brothers Stephen, Damian, and Ky-Mani. Julian's most recent album, Time and Place, was released in 2003. The album's tone was a blend of roots reggae and light jazz. Julian himself stated that the album was another stage in his songwriting evolution that began with Lion in the Morning. Julian forwarded his Rastafarian and frequently aggressive sentiments while the aware and politically charged lyrics of his father and brothers rang in his ears. In keeping with the Marley family tradition, the songs on this album feature a diverse mix of reggae, funk, hip-hop, and rhythm & blues.

Julian, Stephen, and Da-mian created the Time and Place album. Both Ziggy and Rohan contributed percussion lines to the album. Bunny Wailer, Bob's former Wailers bandmate, also contributed some percussion. The Uprising band also contributed to the record. Julian toured in support of the record following its release, and the Uprising band accompanied him. Julian stands out among the Marley children due to his personality, presence, and musical ability. He devotes his time and attention to advancing his father's musical legacy.

Ky-Mani Marley was the result of Bob's liaison with Anita Belnavis. Belnavis was a popular Caribbean table tennis player. Ky-Mani translates to "adventurous traveller," and that is exactly what he has been. Belnavis' life was mostly unreported, but her renowned son is well-known. Ky-Mani Marley was born in Falmouth, Jamaica, and resided there until the age of nine. At the time, he relocated to Miami's inner city, where he spent his time participating in sports. He began studying music as a child, taking piano and guitar classes and playing trumpet in his high school band. Despite studying music, his first interest was athletics, and he participated in high school football and soccer.

Ky-Mani spent his childhood summers with his father, Rita, and the other Marley children. In fact, Ky-Mani relocated to Jamaica in 1992 to be closer to the Marley family. His first foray into music occurred when he was still in Miami. He started rapping and DJing and even released a single called "Unnecessary Badness." Ky-Mani devoted himself to music after returning to Jamaica. He collaborated with Stephen, Julian, and Damian to create his own musical composition.

Ky-Mani recorded numerous tracks on the Shang Records label early in his career. He sang "Judge Not" alongside dancehall queen Patra, which was followed by "Dear Dad." This second song was written as an open letter to his late father. "Dear Dad," a sentimental and thought-provoking song, was an early evidence of Ky-Mani's creative abilities. Ky-Mani was gaining traction when he collaborated with Praswell on a rendition of the Eddy Grant classic "Electric Avenue." Ky-Mani gained significant worldwide attention when she performed at the Midem (Marché international de l'édition musicale), the world's largest music industry trade exhibition. His Midem performance was broadcast live by the Caribbean News Agency, exposing Ky-Mani to an audience of 36 countries.

Ky-Mani's appearance on worldwide television sparked tremendous interest in the young vocalist. Following a label bidding war, Ky-Mani signed with Gee Street/V2 Records. He collaborated with P.M. Dawn on the Gee Street track "Gotta Be Movin' On Up," which only added to Ky-Mani's already growing stock. With the release of his solo first album, Ky-Mani Marley: Like Fa-ther Like Son, in 1999, he heightened interest in his music even further. The Journey, released the following year, demonstrated Ky-Mani's diverse style well. The tracks on the CD are as diverse as Ky-Mani's taste, ranging from Spanish guitar to rock steady to lovers rock.

Ky-Mani's next album, Many More Roads, was released in 2001. The brilliant singer/songwriter performed compositions influenced by roots reggae, dancehall, and rhythm and blues. Ky-Mani preached a message of consciousness throughout this album while remaining true to his Rastafarian ideology.

Ky-Mani's most recent efforts had him dabbling in show industry. He was the lead in the underground Jamaican film Shottas, alongside Wyclef Jean (of the Fugees) and dancehall staple Spragga Benz. He also appeared in the romantic comedy One Love, alongside Cherine Anderson. In 2004, Ky-Mani won another film part, this time as John the Baptist in Frank E. Flow-ers' Haven. The young Rasta appeared opposite Bill Paxton and Orlando Bloom in this film. Ky-Mani is still thrilled about his involvement in preserving Bob's musical fame. He has already done a lot to keep the family name alive, and more effort is on the way.

Apart from Rita, Cindy Breakspeare was the lady most frequently linked with Bob. Breakspeare came from a white, upper-class family and met Bob in the mid-1970s while working in Kingston. She met Bob as a teenager while working at the Kingston Sheraton and living at Blackwell's house at 56 Hope Road. Bob and Shakespeare did not engage much at first. Bob was said to have made numerous attempts to win Shakespeare's favour, but she always turned him down. The song "Waiting in Vain" by Bob was claimed to be about these rejected advertisements. Cindy gradually warmed to Bob's attention as his career grew.

Shakespeare's meteoric climb paralleled Bob's. Breakspeare was a classic beauty who went from Miss Jamaica Bikini to Miss Universe Bikini to Miss World in the mid-1970s. Because of her relationship with Bob, she was also accused of being a homewrecker. However, history shows that Bob pursued Shakespeare and that she was unaware that he was married at the time. The most time the two spent together was during Bob's self-imposed exile from Jamaica following the assassination attempt.

Bob's enthusiasm in Shakespeare ran counter to his philosophy for the rest of his life. Breakspeare was everything that represented

Babylon, in that she hailed from an affluent white family and surrounded herself with vanity issues. As a result, she was more concerned with winning beauty pageants like Miss Jamaica Body Beautiful and Miss Universe Bikini than she was with the suffering of Jamaica's black underclass. Bob, on the other hand, was drawn to her not only sexually, but also because of her honesty. As a result, Bob lavished her with attention that he did not bestow on any other lady. He bought her a house in Kingston's Cherry Gardens neighbourhood and offered her money to start her own business. Unlike his prior relationships, when Bob and Shakespeare's sexual relationship ended, they remained friends for the rest of Bob's life.

Shakespeare later married jazz guitarist and pilot Rupert Bent. They live in Jamaica's Stony Hill neighbourhood, and she is always busy. In addition to her singing profession, through which she met her present husband, she runs the Italian artisan shop that Bob helped her start. Cindy is also the mother of Bob's son, Damian "Junior Gong" Marley. Damian was born in Jamaica in 1978 and has carved out a significant niche in the Jamaican music business. The Junior Gong is the youngest child of any Marley mother.

Damian, like his siblings and sisters, began his musical career at a young age. When he was 13, he created the Shepherds band and began playing. The trio achieved local success and even performed at Reggae Bash in 1992 and Reggae Sunsplash in 1992. Damian frequently performed in front of his elder brothers and sisters as the opening act for Melody Makers performances. Damian was already attempting to develop a solo career by 1994. Mr. Marley, his solo debut album, was released in 1996. Despite the fact that it was a solo album, Damian's brother Stephen appeared on several songs and was the producer. The album was released under the Ghetto Youths International label.

Damian came into his own with his second solo album, Half-way Tree, released in 2001. Damian flexed his now-powerful songwriting abilities on the record, which garnered him a Grammy Award for

Best Reggae record of the Year. The release's major problem was that it was mostly overlooked by the record-buying audience. That all changed in 2005, when Damian published Welcome to Jamrock. This product received tremendous pre-release anticipation and was an instant hit when it hit the streets. The title tune quickly became available in remixes and different versions, and the album charted in the Top 10. The album combined hard-hitting lyrics on life's harsh truths with varied music that incorporated reggae, hip-hop, rhythm and blues, and dancehall.

It was another solo release, however Damian credited Stephen as co-producer. The production technique is similar to that of roots reggae legends Sly and Robbie. The album was published on the family's Tuff Gong/Ghetto Youths International label once more, and it showcased yet another of the Marley children coming into their own. Damian's latest album, in light of his father's legacy, merged songs of protest with songs of love, and once again forwarded Bob's music and message.

Damian's most popular (and thus far most commercially viable) material matched his father's most belligerent sentiments. "Welcome to Jamrock" was a heated and outraged portrayal of the disadvantaged trapped in slavery by Jamaica's government system. This has not gone unnoticed by the younger Marley. Damian has worked long and hard to make his music resonate on the streets, and his most recent efforts have accomplished that goal.

In 1981, the last of the known Marley children was born. Makeda Jahnesta Marley was the result of a chance meeting between Bob Marley and Yvette Crichton. Aside from the famous product, little more was known about this union. The initial name of Bob's youngest child was inspired by the Bible and was also the Ethiopian name for the Queen of Sheba. Her surname is a combination of the Rastafari term for God and her father's middle name. Makeda does not appear to have established a career in the spotlight, and little is known about her other than the fact that by 1992 she had become an official beneficiary of the Marley estate and was a frequent at Rita's residence from then on.

Bob's life took an unusual turn when his death was reported in late 2006. Rita is working on a new Bob Marley film on his life before he became famous. Ra-chid Bouchareb (Dust of Life), an Oscar nominee, has been chosen to direct the film. The main source of dispute has been Rita's choice of Jamie Foxx to play the young Bob. While Foxx was praised for his portrayal of Ray Charles, he is unlikely to pull off a 16-year-old Marley. The film has already received harsh criticism as a result of this questionable decision, despite the fact that it has only recently begun pre-production in early 2007.

Even so, the legend lives on. Bob's name, in addition to his popularity, legacy, children, and music, is still honoured and celebrated. The man's memory continues to pique people's interest around the world. Every year, international concerts are held to commemorate his birthday. Contrary to popular belief, the concerts continue to expand in size and popularity, with more and more people attending each year.

One particularly fascinating example was Bob's 60th birthday celebration in 2005. The official, and largest, celebration was held in Addis Ababa, Ethiopia, and was accompanied by a three-day conference dedicated to all things Bob. Members of the Ethiopian government, Madame Winnie Mandela, Cedella Marley, Maya Angelou, India Irie, Ziggy Marley, and Angelique Kidjo were among those who took part in the conference. Baaba Maal, Youssou N'Dour, An-gelique Kidjo, Tagass King, and Rita and Ziggy Marley were among the performers who graced the stage during the event. The meeting in Ethiopia was the focal point of the event, but there were parallel festivities all over the world. The Bob Marley Foundation organised celebrations for Bob Marley's 60th birthday in the United States, Italy, Sweden, Germany, and South Africa.

Another significant event was Bob Marley's 62nd birthday celebration in 2007. On February 10, Stephen, Julian, Damian, and Ky-Mani put on a concert dubbed "Smile Jamaica." The performance was held at the ancestral home of Bob Marley in Nine Mile, St. Ann Parish, Jamaica. The name of the show was inspired by a similar performance given by their father in 1976. Bob was spreading the message of peace at that first concert, and his sons have continued that objective. The event was planned to coincide with Bob Marley week, when the most tourists visit Jamaica. With this, the joy and message of Bob's life and music are carried on. His children will carry on his legacy, and he will not be forgotten. From Nine Mile to Kingston, from Miami to New York, from Jamaica to the rest of the world, Robert Nesta Marley's music lives on.

The contents of this book may not be copied, reproduced or transmitted without the express written permission of the author or publisher. Under no circumstances will the publisher or author be responsible or liable for any damages, compensation or monetary loss arising from the information contained in this book, whether directly or indirectly. .

Disclaimer Notice:

Although the author and publisher have made every effort to ensure the accuracy and completeness of the content, they do not, however, make any representations or warranties as to the accuracy, completeness, or reliability of the content. , suitability or availability of the information, products, services or related graphics contained in the book for any purpose. Readers are solely responsible for their use of the information contained in this book

Every effort has been made to make this book possible. If any omission or error has occurred unintentionally, the author and publisher will be happy to acknowledge it in upcoming versions.

Copyright © 2023

All rights reserved.

Printed in Great Britain
by Amazon